Essential
French
Riviera

by Teresa Fisher

Above: *fishing boats enhance the old port at Menton, France's warmest resort*

PASSPORT BOOKS

NTC/Contemporary Publishing Group

Above: *Even the locals find time to enjoy the sunshine*

Front cover: *Jardin Exotique, Monaco; Provençal dolls; dressed for the sun*
Back cover: *bakery, Antibes*

Published by Passport Books, a division of NTC/Contemporary Publishing Group, Inc. 4255 West Touhy Avenue, Lincolnwood (Chicago), Illinois 60646-1975, U.S.A.

Published by Passport Books in conjunction with The Automobile Association of Great Britain.

Written by Teresa Fisher

Library of Congress Catalog Card Number: 98-68310
ISBN 0-8442-2200-3

Color separation: Pace Colour, Southampton

Printed and bound in Italy by Printer Trento srl

Contents

About this Book

KEY TO SYMBOLS

✚ map reference to the maps found in the What to See section (below)

✉ address or location

☎ telephone number

🕐 opening times

🍴 restaurant or café on premises or near by

Ⓜ nearest underground train station

🚌 nearest bus/tram route

🚆 nearest overground train station

🚢 ferry crossings and boat excursions

✈ travel by air

ℹ tourist information

♿ facilities for visitors with disabilities

✋ admission charge

↔ other places of interest near by

❓ other practical information

➤ indicates the page where you will find a fuller description

Essential *French Riviera* is divided into five sections to cover the most important aspects of your visit to the French Riviera.

Viewing the French Riviera pages 5–14
An introduction to the region by the author.
Features of the French Riviera
Essence of the French Riviera
The Shaping of the French Riviera
Peace and Quiet
Famous of the French Riviera

Top Ten pages 15–26
The author's choice of the Top Ten places to see in the French Riviera, in alphabetical order, each with practical information.

What to See pages 27–90
Nice and the rest of the French Riviera, each with brief introductions and an alphabetical listing of the main attractions.
Practical information
Snippets of 'Did you know…' information
4 suggested walks
4 suggested tours
2 features

Where To… pages 91–116
Detailed listings of the best places to eat, stay, shop, take the children and be entertained.

Practical Matters pages 117–124
A highly visual section containing essential travel information.

Maps
All map references are to the individual maps found in the What to See section of this guide.

For example, St-Tropez has the reference ✚ 65B2 – indicating the page on which the map is located and the grid square in which St-Tropez is to be found. A list of the maps that have been used in this travel guide can be found in the index.

Prices
Where appropriate, an indication of the cost of an establishment is given by £ signs: £££ denotes higher prices, ££ denotes average prices, while £ denotes lower charges.

Star Ratings
Most of the places described in this book have been given a separate rating:

✪✪✪ Do not miss
✪✪   Highly recommended
✪   Worth seeing

Viewing the
French
Riviera

Above: *sunflowers nodding in the sun*
Right: *guarding the palace at Monaco*

Teresa Fisher's French Riviera

The Riviera

From Menton on the Italian border to the popular fishing port and resort of le Lavandou, the French Riviera packs a surprising amount into a small area, encompassing a string of smart resorts, beautiful peninsulas sprinkled with sumptuous villas amidst sub-tropical foliage, wooded islets temptingly close to the sandy shoreline and three mountain ranges: the Alpes-Maritimes, the brick-red Massif de l'Esterel and the ancient chestnut-forested Massif des Maures.

Top up your tan on the beach at Cannes by day (below), or shop in the glamorous streets of Antibes into the night (above)

Ever since the poet Stephen Liégeard visited the Riviera in 1887 and exclaimed 'Côte d'Azur!', this dramatic stretch of azure coast with its chic resorts, fishing villages, sandy beaches, and craggy corniches has attracted a rich assortment of actors, artists, writers, film stars

and royalty. For this is the home of the rich and famous, the cradle of impressionism, the home of the bikini and the world's most sophisticated holiday playground.

But what is so magical about the Riviera that it should draw millions of devotees back year after year for their annual fix of heady, Mediterranean *joie de vivre*? Is it the luxury hotels, designer shops, palm-lined promenades and terrace cafés of the exclusive resorts – Nice, Cannes, Monaco and St-Tropez – which bask in the scorching Mediterranean sun, with their 'see-and-be-seen' ports overflowing with millionaires' yachts; or perhaps the thrill of a casino; or the glamorous sun-soaked beaches?

For me, the Riviera is all this and much, much more. For there is another side to the region that is easy to miss – a *douceur de vivre* that is hard to imagine in the midst of the coast-courting tourist hordes. Head inland to the hidden valleys and wild Alpine scenery, where the air is fragrant with the perfumes of Provence, to discover a great wealth of sleepy villages among countryside painted with all the vivid colours of Picasso, Renoir and Matisse.

The Riviera is a region of great contrasts that caters for all tastes with an endless choice of enticing destinations, a robust local cuisine and an exceptional heritage. Combine all this with a climate that boasts 300 days of sunshine a year, and who can resist a holiday here?

Features of the French Riviera

Language
- In some tourist centres, English threatens to become the *lingua franca* while a revival of traditional Provençal language – *langue d'oc* – is taking place in the hinterland.

Location
- The Riviera, from Menton on the Italian border to le Lavandou, is squeezed on to a narrow strip of coastland between the Mediterranean and the Alpes-Maritimes.

Climate
- Typically Mediterranean, with approximately 300 days of sunshine a year. The best times to visit are May, June and September, avoiding the crowds of July and August.
- Although originally a winter resort, it can get cold and wet during these months, with snow in the Alps and a biting *mistral* wind of up to 290kph.

Economy
- Nice is the capital of the Alpes-Maritimes *département*, and its airport is the second busiest in the land.
- Thanks to popular resorts such as Cannes and St-Tropez, tourism is the region's main money-spinner.
- Monaco is a world-famous financial centre and tax haven.
- North of Cannes, France's 'Silicon Valley' – the Sophia-Antipolis business park – is regarded as the technological heart of southern Europe, containing over 1,000 enterprises employing 20,000-plus people.

The Principality of Monaco
- **Size** – 195ha (including 31ha reclaimed from the sea)
- **Population** – 30,000 (including 6,000 Monégasques)
- **Currency** – French franc
- **Religion** – Catholicism
- **National Holiday** – 19 November
- **Access** – 22km from Nice-Côte d'Azur Airport
- **Constitution** – Hereditary monarchy with the Prince as Head of State
- **Current Ruler** – His Serene Highness Prince Rainier III

Street cafés – at the heart of Riviera lifestyle

Essence of the French Riviera

Why does the Riviera remain so popular with connoisseurs of the good things in life, and those who could afford to live and holiday anywhere in the world? Some come for the exceptionally mild winters or the grandeur of the rugged coast. Others favour the art treasures, the ancient ruins and the sleepy villages. Many more come simply for the glamour of the seaside resorts. The charms of the Riviera are so varied that most visitors are at a loss to know where to start. First-time visitors soon fall under the region's spell while those who already know it remain enchanted, returning year after year.

Lazy days in the sun ... but remember your parasol!

THE 10 ESSENTIALS

If you have only a short time to visit the Riviera, or would like to get a really complete picture of the region, here are the essentials:

- **Bask in the sun on one of the Riviera's sandy beaches**, or relax under the shade of a classic striped parasol.
- **Visit the Cours Saleya market in Nice** (➤ 36), and treat yourself to a picnic of goat's cheese, tomatoes, olives and local wine.
- **Promenade the water-front at St-Tropez** (➤ 80) in your finery, admiring its ostentatious yachts and gin palaces (…and don't forget your trendy sunglasses!).
- **Visit some of France's finest modern art galleries**: Fondation Maeght (➤ 20), Musée Matisse (➤ 23), Musée Picasso (➤ 25), Musée Renoir (➤ 52), Musée de l'Annonciade (➤ 83).
- **Dine in one of Mougins' world-class restaurants** (➤ 97), and marvel at the enticing tastes, fragrances and colours of Provençal cuisine.
- **Try a little gambling** at the world-famous Casino de Monte-Carlo (➤ 16).
- **Join the laid-back locals in a game of *boules*** – this ancient game originated here and, although now played throughout the world, the most fiercely contested games still take place in the shady village squares of the French Riviera.
- **Spot the rich and famous at the Cannes Film Festival**, the glitziest, most glamorous event on the Côte d'Azur.
- **Escape the frenetic coastal resorts** and explore the sleepy surrounding countryside, dotted with *villages perchés*.
- **Create your very own scent** at one of Grasse's many perfumeries (➤ 61).

St-Tropez – ritzy port of call

A game of boules *is enjoyable for both players and spectators*

The Shaping of the French Riviera

c900 BC
First signs of human settlement.

500–400 BC
Greeks set up trading posts at St-Tropez, Antibes, Nice and Monaco.

c300 BC
Celtic invasions of Provence and Côte d'Azur.

125 BC
Romans conquer southern Gaul and name it Provincia.

58–52 BC
Caesar's conquest of Gaul.

6 BC
Alpine Trophy at la Turbie constructed.

476
Fall of Roman Empire. The Riviera becomes part of the Visigothic Kingdom of Italy.

536
The Riviera comes under Frankish rule.

8–10th century
Saracens invade southern France; the Riviera becomes part of the Carolingian Empire.

1032
Provence becomes part of Holy Roman Empire.

1297
Francesco 'the Spiteful' seizes Monaco for the Grimaldi family.

1308
A member of the Grimaldi family purchases the estate of Monaco from the Genoese.

1388
Nice hands itself over to the Count of Savoy.

1450s
The first Nice School of painters is formed; fine Renaissance altarpieces created in many of the region's churches.

1691
Nice occupied by the French, but returned to Savoy in 1696.

1720
Great Plague kills over 100,000 people.

1793
Nice is reunited with France.

1799
Napoléon lands at St-Raphaël on his return from Egypt.

1814
Napoléon leaves St-Raphaël for the island of Elba.

The Roman Trophée des Alpes at la Turbie

1815
Napoléon returns from Elba, landing at Golfe Juan.

1830s
Beginnings of tourism on the French Riviera.

1848
Menton and Roquebrune successfully revolt against Grimaldi rule from Monaco.

1860
Nice votes to join France.

1865
Monte-Carlo is founded and the first casino opens.

1878
Development of a winter tourist season on the Riviera.

Late 19th century
St-Tropez School of painting founded.

1902
First Monte-Carlo Rally.

1908
Renoir moves to the Riviera, where he lives until his death in 1919.

1917
Matisse settles in Nice, and stays until his death in 1955.

1920s–30s
Riviera becomes fashionable, achieving status as an international summer resort.

1940
The Italians occupy Menton.

1942
Nazis invade southern France.

1944
Allied troops liberate Provence and the Côte d'Azur.

1947
Picasso moves to Antibes.

1947
The First International Film Festival is held at Cannes.

1949
Prince Rainier III of Monaco accedes to the throne, and in 1956 marries American actress Grace Kelly.

1959
Floods in Fréjus kill 421.

1962
Algerian war of independence; many French North Africans (*pieds-noirs*) settle on the Riviera. Nice-Côte d'Azur Airport opens.

1970
Autoroute du Soleil completed.

1980s
Extreme right political parties gain popularity in key coastal cities.

1982
Princess Grace is killed in a car crash on the Moyenne Corniche above Monaco. Graham Greene publishes a pamphlet on organised crime on the French Riviera called *J'Accuse: The Dark Side of Nice*.

1989
Law passed to toughen measures against forest fires, which pose an increasing threat to the region.

1990
Under indictment for misuse of public funds, Nice's right-wing mayor, Jacques Médecin, flees to Uruguay to avoid trial for corruption.

1997
700th anniversary of the Grimaldi dynasty in Monaco.

The 1920s on the Riviera – popular then as now

Peace & Quiet

Despite the Riviera's popularity, it is still possible to escape the bustling coastal resorts and discover the region's hidden delights. Wander through the fields and forests, hike in the hills, gorges and mountains or stroll along the shoreline and you will be amazed by the vast array of flora and fauna in surprisingly varied habitats.

The Coast

Perhaps the most startling contrasts are along the coast, which encompasses the jagged rocky inlets of the blood-red Massif de l'Esterel (► 17), the majestic bays that have made Nice and Cannes famous, and the dramatic shoreline further east, where seabirds and birds of prey soar above cliffs that drop precipitously into the sea. The exotic palm trees, mimosas, eucalpytus and succulents, so intrinsic to the coastal landscape today, were imported by wintering holidaymakers only a century or two ago.

Sweet chestnuts in the Massif des Maures

The coast supports a colourful bird life, in particular the bright yellow serins and Sardinian warblers of the rocky Esterel and there is an abundance of marine creatures, many of which feature in the cuisine of Provence. A total of 638 species of fish have been registered here, with scorpionfish, gilthead and hog-fish (the basis of *bouillabaisse*) particularly prized by fishermen.

Off the Îles de Lérins (► 21), it is possible to swim in the sea alongside vividly coloured fish (sea peacocks, black-faced blennies), while octopuses, jellyfish, starfish and shimmering pastel-coloured sea slugs lurk amongst beds of Neptune grass, sponges, sea anemones and abundant corals.

The Hinterland

One of the joys of a holiday on the Riviera is the opportunity to discover its unspoilt hinterland. A special delight is to ramble through the region's extensive scrub habitat (locally called *maquis*) of heather, gorse and mimosa, all flecked with wild flowers. The fragrance of *herbes de Provence* – rosemary, thyme, basil, marjoram and tarragon – fills the warm air, and only the sound of bees, grasshoppers and crickets disturbs the peace.

The region's sunshine and favourable climate allow many interesting trees to thrive, including olives, parasol pines, almonds, an abundance of fruit trees and neat, ubiquitous rows of tall cypresses. The shade of the cork

oak and chestnut woodlands of the Massif des Maures
(► 63) provides welcome relief from the midday heat and
sanctuary for bee-eaters, shrikes, hoopoes and the rare
Hermanns tortoise.

The Mountains

It is easy to forget that the Riviera comprises as much
mountain as coast. Behind Cannes and Antibes, undulating
hills stretch to the Pré-Alpes of Grasse, cut by dramatic
ravines and gorges such as the Gorges du Loup (► 88)
and carpeted with acre upon acre of flowers – jasmine,
roses, carnations and striped fields of lavender, stretching
like mauve corduroy across the countryside.

Further east, the Vallée de la Vésubie in the Pré-Alpes
of Nice offers walkers and bird watchers spectacular alpine
scenery and occasional glimpses of rare birds. A short
journey north leads to the majestic, snow-capped peaks of
the Alpes-Maritimes and the Parc National du Mercantour,
the only remaining French National State Park, ablaze with
rhododendrons and gentians in spring; it boasts 600km of
designated footpaths amid chamois, ibex, wild sheep and
marmots and with breathtaking alpine views.

*The Parc National du
Mercantour is a region of
unspoiled wilderness and
imposing peaks*

Famous of the French Riviera

Coco Chanel – Riviera trend-setter

Ever since the mid-19th century, when two Englishmen – Tobias Smollett and Henry Lord Brougham – 'discovered' this then wild and isolated stretch of coastline squeezed between the Alps and the Mediterranean, a rich assortment of artists, writers, philosophers, movie stars and royalty has been captivated by the French Riviera.

Queen Victoria, Napoléon, Brigitte Bardot, Boris Becker, and more recently the late Princess Diana and Dodi Al Fayed – have all been seduced by the beauty of the landscape and the sparkling azure sea. As Nietzsche wrote in 1883: 'Here, the days follow on with a beauty that I would describe as almost insolent. I have never lived through a winter of such constant perfection.'

Initially, the Riviera was a sedate winter resort for English and Russian nobility. It was not until the 1930s that it became a summer resort, when Coco Chanel made suntans fashionable and when trend-setting Americans including Harpo Marx, Cole Porter, Isadora Duncan – who tragically died in Nice when her scarf became entangled round the axle of her open car (➤ 37) – and F Scott Fitzgerald gave the Côte d'Azur its racy, glamorous image.

Many writers have been drawn to the Riviera over the years, and it has been the focus of countless literary masterpieces. However, it is the innumerable great artists who have left the deepest imprint on the region. As Van Gogh remarked on moving to Provence, 'The future of modern art lies in the South of France'. Over the years, Renoir, Dufy, Matisse, Picasso, to name but a few, have immortalised the region's most beautiful sites on canvas, hypnotised by the rich palette of landscapes and the almost magical, incandescent light that has provided inspiration over the centuries – as it still does today for a new generation of artists and writers.

Star-spotting

The Riviera is currently home to Brigitte Bardot, Joan Collins, Mick Jagger, Elton John, Steffi Graf, Karl Lagerfeld, Roger Moore and a whole host of celebrities. The coast continues to attract megastars including Sylvester Stallone, Claudia Schiffer and Sharon Stone. Best star-spotting venues include the Cannes International Film Festival, the St-Tropez waterfront and beaches, shops in Monaco, restaurants in Mougins or, just like in the movies, along the Corniches in an open-top roadster.

Top Ten

Above: *try your luck at the gaming tables*
Right: *a Giacometti piece at Fondation Maeght, St-Paul-de-Vence*

15

1

Casino, Monte-Carlo

The world's most famous casino symbolises all that is opulent and glamorous in Monte-Carlo – a must-see, even if you are not a gambler.

✚ 72C2

✉ place du Casino

☎ 377/92 16 21 21

🕐 Casino: daily from noon (except 1 May). European Rooms from 2PM; Private Rooms from 3PM; English Club from 10PM. Salle Garnier: open only for performances

🍴 Bar and restaurants (£££)

🚌 Monaco/Monte-Carlo

♿ Very good

✋ F50 day/F120 week/ F250 month/F350 season

❓ No persons under 21. Passport required. Jacket and tie recommended

Glitzy Monte-Carlo was built on the back of its world-famous casino

The Casino de Monte-Carlo is probably the most famous building on the French Riviera, known in its heyday as the 'Cathedral of Hell'. It was opened in 1878 by Prince Charles III (after whom Monte-Carlo is named), to save himself from bankruptcy. Such was its success that, five years later, he abolished taxation.

The resplendent building was designed by Charles Garnier, architect of the Paris Opéra. Its lavish *belle-epoque* interior is a riot of pink, green and gold, with marble floors, bronze sculptures, onyx columns and highly ornate ceilings, lit by crystal chandeliers. Note the painted ceiling of the Pink Salon Bar depicting female nudes smoking cigars. It was here in 1891 that Charles Deville Wells turned $400 into $40,000 in a three-day gambling spree, thus inspiring the popular tune 'The Man Who Broke the Bank at Monte-Carlo'.

Ever since, bronzed, bejewelled gamblers have come here from all over the world to try their luck at the gaming tables. Yet gone are the days when the Monégasques could live entirely off the folly of others. Revenue from the Casino has declined, so that now it is worth much more as a tourist attraction.

The Casino building also houses the Salle Garnier, a small but highly ornate opera house, which, for more than a century, has welcomed the world's greatest artists.

2
Corniche d'Or

Edging a wild massif of blood–red porphyry mountains, the 'golden coast road' passes some of the Riviera's most grandiose scenery.

The Corniche d'Or follows the dramatic shoreline from St-Raphaël to Théoule-sur-Mer, along the sole stretch of Riviera coastline that is still virtually untouched by property development. The tortuous road is punctuated by viewpoints overlooking inviting beaches, sheltered yacht harbours, jagged inlets and deserted coves cut by rocky promontories. The Massif de l'Esterel provides a perfect backdrop, with its harsh, rugged mountains of brilliant red volcanic rock jutting out into the sea.

Travelling from east to west, start at Théoule-sur-Mer, a small seaside resort at the rim of the Parc Forestier de la Pointe de l'Aiguille, an extensive coastal park offering a variety of scenic walking trails. There are plenty of hiking possibilities into the Massif de l'Esterel from the coast road. A quick climb along the Pointe de l'Esquillon at Miramar is rewarded by spectacular views of Cap Roux further along the coast.

Le Trayas is located at the highest point of the Corniche. Just beyond, a strenuous inland trail climbs the Pic du Cap Roux. The road continues to twist and turn westwards to St-Raphaël via Anthéor and Agay, the Esterel's main resort; this beautifully situated around a deep horseshoe bay, considered one of the best anchorages on this stretch of coast.

Heading inland from Fréjus, the N7 road to Cannes follows the path of the Roman Via Aurelia through extensive cork forests past Mont Vinaigre (614m), the highest peak in the Esterel. A short path leads to its summit, for an overview of the wilderness that for centuries was a popular haunt of brigands and a refuge for hermits and escaped galley-slaves from Toulon.

✚ 65C3

🍴 Restaurants, bars and cafés (£–£££)

ℹ️ Mandelieu: avenue de Cannes ☎ 04 93 49 14 39; St-Raphaël: place de la Gare ☎ 04 94 19 52 52

↔️ Cannes (➤ 53); Fréjus (➤ 58); Îles de Lérins (➤ 21); St-Raphaël (➤ 79)

❓ Five trains and half-hourly buses travel from Cannes to St-Raphaël daily. Check timetables for details

The azure sea complements the cliffs of the Corniche d'Or

3
Èze

72B2

Restaurants, bars and cafés (£–£££)

Èze: place de Gaulle
☎ 04 93 41 26 00

None

Beaulieu-sur-Mer
(► 50); Cap Ferrat
(► 56); the Corniches
(► 56); Monaco
(► 69); Nice (► 32)

The steep climb to Èze's tropical garden is rewarded by magnificent views

Without doubt one of the Riviera's most strikingly situated and best-preserved perched villages, Èze affords truly breathtaking views.

Èze is frequently called the Nid d'Aigle (Eagle's Nest) because of its remarkable location, perched at the summit of a rocky outcrop, halfway between Nice and Monaco, where the mountains meet the coast.

The settlement records of Èze date back as far as the 11th century although the site has been occupied since the Bronze Age. The village was fortified in the 12th century and belonged to the Counts of Savoy for hundreds of years. In 1792, following the creation of the Alpes-Maritimes, Èze became part of the Principality of Monaco. It was only after the plebiscite of 1860, when locals voted in the village chapel for annexation to France, that peace finally came to Èze.

Top: *it's easy to see why the village is dubbed the 'Eagle's Nest'*

On entering through the only gateway in the ancient ramparts, you will be struck by the tall, golden houses and the labyrinth of tiny vaulted passages with cobbled alleys, which climb steeply up to the ruins of a once massive Saracen fortress 429m above sea level. It is surrounded by an **exotic garden**, bristling with magnificent cacti, succulents and rare palms.

Be sure to take time to explore the *bijou* flower-filled passageways, chock-a-block with countless craft shops hidden in caves within the rock – tiny treasure troves of antiques, ceramics, pewter and olivewood. At the foot of the hill, two Grassois perfume factories, Galimard and Fragonard, contain interesting museums in which the secrets of perfume production are explained. Near by, the Chemin de Nietzsche (a narrow path once frequented by the German philosopher) zigzags steeply down to the beach and the former fishing village of Èze-Bord-de-Mer, now a popular coastal resort.

Jardin Exotique

✉ rue du Château

☎ 04 93 41 10 30

🕐 9–12, 2–dusk

✋ Moderate

Above: *a village of tempting Provençal perfumes ... and exotic plants*

1

4

Fondation Maeght, St–Paul–de–Vence

Hidden amidst umbrella pines above the village of St–Paul–de–Vence, this is one of the world's most distinguished modern art museums.

🕂 57C4

✉ 06570 St-Paul-de-Vence

☎ 04 93 32 09 79

🕓 Oct–Jun 10–12:30, 2:30–6; Jul–Sep 10–7

🍴 Café (£)

ℹ St-Paul-de-Vence: Maison de la tour, 2 rue Grande ☎ 04 93 32 86 95

♿ Few

✋ Very expensive

↔ Vence (► 89)

❓ Gift shop, cinema and art library

Typical Giacometti sculpture in the courtyard

The Maeght Foundation is no ordinary museum. At its inauguration in 1964, André Malraux, Minister of Cultural Affairs, described it as 'a world in which modern art can both find its place and that otherworldliness which used to be called supernatural'.

The foundation was the brainchild of Aimé and Marguerite Maeght, who were art dealers and close friends of many artists, including Matisse, Miró, Braque, Bonnard and Chagall, and it was their private collection that formed the basis of the museum. Their aim was to create a living home for creation with accommodation for artists, and the ideal environment in which to display contemporary art. To achieve this, they worked in close collaboration with Catalan architect José-Luis Sert, a former pupil of Le Corbusier.

The resulting buildings blend artfully into the natural surroundings, respecting the curves of the landscape, and incorporating beautiful terraces, gardens and ponds where contemporary artists have given free rein to their inspiration. Look out for Miró's *Labyrinthe* – a fantastic multi-level maze of mosaics, sculptures, fountains, trees and ceramics; Chagall's vast, joyful canvas *La Vie*; and Cour Giacometti – a tiled courtyard peopled with skinny Giacometti figures. There is also a chapel in the grounds, built in memory of the Maeghts' son who died in 1953 aged 11, which contains striking stained-glass windows by Braque and Ubac.

Inside the museum, the remarkable permanent collection consists exclusively of 20th-century art and includes works by nearly every major artist of the past 50 years; these are displayed on a rotation basis throughout the year, except during summer, when temporary exhibitions are held.

5
Îles de Lérins

Take refuge from crowded Cannes on these two tiny islands, perfect for a stroll, a swim and a picnic, or to visit their important religious sites.

The charming, car-free Îles de Lérins lie just 15 minutes by ferry from Cannes. They are named after two saints – Saint Honorat, who founded a monastery on the smaller of the two islands at the end of the 4th century, and his sister Sainte Marguerite, who set up a nunnery on the other island – and were once the most powerful ecclesiastical centres in the south of France.

Île Ste-Marguerite is the largest of the islands. Its main attraction is undoubtedly the **Fort Royal**, which contains the Musée de la Mer (Maritime Museum), with Ligurian, Greek and Roman artefacts excavated on the island alongside objects recovered from ships sunk off its shores.

The fort was built under Richelieu, strengthened by Vauban in 1712, then restored under Napoléon. Used as a prison from 1685 until the early 20th century, its most illustrious occupant (from 1687 to 1698) was the mysterious 'Man in the Iron Mask' whose identity is still unknown.

Île St-Honorat maintains an active monastery. The 19th-century Abbaye de Lérins is open daily to visitors, and the Cistercian monks produce lavender, oranges, honey and a sweet liqueur, made from aromatic Provençal plants.

Both islands offer pleasant walking trails. One of the most enjoyable is a shaded route round Île St-Honorat, past the seven chapels scattered across the island, of which Chapelle de la Trinité and Chapelle Sainte-Croix are particularly interesting.

✝ 57B1

🍴 Restaurants and cafés (££)

🚢 Compagnie Maritime Cannoise ☎ 04 93 38 66 33. Ferry crossings daily in summer, 7:30–4:15. Restricted service in winter. Journey times: St-Honorat 30 minutes; Ste-Marguerite 15 minutes

ℹ️ Cannes: Palais des Festivals, 1 la Croisette ☎ 04 93 99 19 77

🖐 Ste-Marguerite: F40; St-Honorat: F45; combined ticket: F60

Fort Royal

✉️ Île Ste-Marguerite

☎ 04 93 43 18 17

🕐 Summer: 10:30–12, 2–6:30; winter: varies

♿ Few 🖐 Cheap

Île-Ste-Marguerite is popular for diving and bathing

6
MAMAC, Nice

🕂 33E2

✉ promenade des Arts

☎ 04 93 62 61 62

🕐 11–6 (till 10 Fri). Closed Tue and hols

🍴 Café and restaurant (££)

🚌 1, 2, 3, 4, 5, 6, 7, 9, 10, 14, 16, 17, 25

🚆 Nice

ℹ avenue Thiers (Gare SNCF) ☎ 04 93 87 07 07

♿ Excellent

✋ Expensive

❓ Shop. Auditorium showing art videos

MAMAC's huge, light galleries provide the perfect setting for 'living art'

The remarkable Musée d'Art Moderne et d'Art Contemporain traces the history of French and American avant-garde from the 1960s.

MAMAC was inaugurated in 1990 as a vast monument to the ambitions of the city's former National Front leader, Jacques Médecin. Even the building, designed by Yves Bayard and Henri Vidal, is a masterpiece of modern art with its four octagonal, grey-marble towers linked together by glassed-in walkways.

MAMAC's collections are exhibited in rotation and reflect the main avant-garde art movements of the last 40 years in France and the US. The primary focus is on French neo-realism and the artists of the second École de Nice, featuring works by Rayasse, César, Arman, Ben, Tinguely, and Yves Klein. Many of their works involve smashing, tearing, burning or distorting mundane objects of everyday life as a spoof on society and the highbrow art world.

Look out also for artists of the *support-surface* movement (who sought to reduce painting to its material-istic reality, concentrating on the frame and the texture of the canvas) and the graffiti-obsesssed 'fluxus' movement, best portrayed in the fun, push-button Little Shop of Ben. American abstraction, minimalism and pop art are also well represented. Highlights include several Lichtenstein cartoons and Warhol's famous Campbell's soup tin.

No visit to MAMAC would be complete without visiting the rooftop terraces for unsurpassed views of Nice. Here on Fridays at 9:30PM, the illumi-nation of Klein's *Mur de Feu* (Wall of Fire) is a unique spectacle.

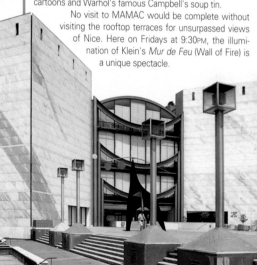

7
Musée Matisse, Nice

Here in this handsome villa is a remarkable collection – a visual history of Matisse's works that spans his entire life and appeals to everyone.

The vivid-red façade of the Musée Matisse

Henri Matisse came to live in Nice in 1917 and, shortly before his death in 1954, he bequeathed his entire personal collection to the city. Together with a second, even bigger, donation from his wife in 1960 (including over 100 personal effects from his studio in the nearby Hôtel Regina), it formed the basis of a priceless collection that celebrates the life, work and influence of this great artist.

This worthy collection is housed in a striking mid-17th-century villa with a cleverly painted *trompe-l'oeil* façade, colonnaded staircases and Italianate terraces, all set in the midst of a large olive grove on a hill in the Cimiez district of Nice (➤ 35).

The museum allows visitors an overview of Matisse's entire working life, starting with copies of Old Master paintings that he made during his apprenticeship, through an era of sober, dark-toned paintings of the 1890s (including his first personal painting, *Nature Morte aux Livres*, and *Intérieur à l'Harmonium*), his impressionist and fauvist phases (*Jeune Femme à l'Ombrelle* and *Portrait of Madame Matisse*), to the bright colours and simple shapes of his maturity, best portrayed in his decorative post-war paper cut-outs, silk-screen hangings, and works such as *Nu Bleu IV* and *Nature Morte aux Grenades*.

The museum also boasts all the bronze sculptures that Matisse ever made, and the world's largest collection of his drawings and engravings, including his illustrations for James Joyce's novel *Ulysses*, and his powerful sketches and stained-glass models for the remarkable Chapelle du Rosaire at Vence (➤ 89). There are also three temporary exhibitions held every year.

✝ 33E5

✉ 164 avenue des Arènes-de-Cimiez

☎ 04 93 81 08 08

🕐 Apr–Sep 10–6; Oct–Mar 10–5. Closed Tue and hols

🚌 15, 17, 20, 22, 25

🚆 Nice

♿ Very good

✋ Expensive

❓ Guided tours Wed 3PM except during school hols

8
Musée Océanographique, Monaco

Perched high on a sheer cliff, this museum of marine science with its spectacular aquarium is the finest of its kind.

 72C2

✉ avenue St-Martin, Monaco-Ville

☎ 377/193 15 36 00

🕐 Oct–Mar 9:30–7; Apr–Jun, Sep 9–7; Jul–Aug 9–8; Nov–Feb 10–6. Closed 19 May

🍴 Restaurant and bar (££)

🚌 Monaco

ℹ 2a boulevard des Moulins ☎ 377/92 16 61 16

♿ Very good

✋ Very expensive

❓ Jacques Cousteau films shown Thu–Tue at 2:30 and 4. Mediterranean satellite film half-past every hour from 9:30–6:30 taken by Meteosat 36,000km away

Monaco's prestigious Oceanographic Museum was founded in 1910 by Prince Albert I, who was a keen oceanographer, as an institute for scientific research and to house the many marine specimens he collected on his numerous voyages.

Financed by profits from the Casino, it took 11 years and 100,000 tons of white stone from la Turbie (➤ 73) to build. The resulting edifice, with its staggering 85m sheer façade that plunges straight into the sea, is a masterpiece of monumental architecture.

The museum contains some exceptional collections of nautical instruments, marine flora and fauna, including the skeletons of a 20m whale and a 200kg giant turtle; models of all the magnificent ships built for the sovereign's voyages, along with the laboratory installed in his last boat, *Hirondelle II*; displays demonstrating natural sea phenomena such as waves, tides, currents and salinity; and the world's first submarine.

The basement houses the famed Aquarium, which exhibits thousands of rare fish with beautifully lit displays of living corals from all over the world, in 90 tanks with a direct supply of sea water. Don't miss the Pacific black-tipped sharks, the Australian leafy seadragons, the shimmering sea slugs, the luminous yellow sturgeon, the sinister black lantern-eye fish (aptly nicknamed 'demons of the night') and, if you are able to spot them, the cunningly camouflaged marine chameleons.

The remainder of the building contains research laboratories specialising in the study of ocean pollution and radioactivity that, until recently, were headed by marine explorer Jacques Cousteau. His remarkable films are regularly screened in the museum's cinema.

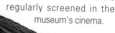

Fish of many colours – like this angel fish – dazzle visitors to the Océanographic Museum

9

Musée Picasso, Antibes

Picasso once had a studio inside Antibes' old, seafront Château Grimaldi. Today it houses one of the world's finest collections of his works.

The former fortress of the Grimaldi family

The Grimaldi family ruled for centuries from this beautiful 13th- to 16th-century castle, constructed following the design of an ancient Roman fort. In 1928, the city of Antibes bought the castle to house its Museum of Art, History and Archaeology. When Pablo Picasso returned to his beloved Mediterranean in 1946, after spending the war years in Paris, he found that he had nowhere suitable to work so the Mayor of Antibes lent him a room in Château Grimaldi.

After the melancholy of war, Picasso's work here took on a new dimension, reflecting the *joie de vivre* of the Mediterranean, bathed in sunny colours and incandescent light. He combined his bold new techniques with ancient themes and mythical images, creating such masterpieces as *Le Centaur et le Navire*, *Ulysée et les Sirènes*, *Nu Couché au Lit Bleu* and his famous *Antipolis* or *La Joie de Vivre*.

Although Picasso spent only six months working here, it was one of his most prolific phases. In gratitude, he donated the complete works of this period to the castle museum, together with a lively collection of tapestries, sculptures and over 150 ceramics designed at nearby Vallauris (► 49).

Most of Picasso's works can be found on the first floor of the castle, while the ground floor contains photographs of the great master at work. Works by his contemporaries, including Léger, Ernst and Hartung, hang on the second floor in Picasso's former studio, and the sunny terrace overhanging the Mediterranean provides an amusing location for stone and bronze sculptures by Miró, Richier and Pagès, displayed amongst cacti, trees and flowers.

✚ 29D2

✉ Château Grimaldi

☎ 04 92 90 54 20

🕐 Jun–Sep 10–6; Oct–May 10–12, 2–6. Closed Mon and hols

🚌 Antibes

♿ Good

✋ Expensive

❓ Guided tours on request. Children's workshops

10
Villa Ephrussi de Rothschild, St-Jean-Cap-Ferrat

🕂 72B1

✉ chemin du Musée, St-Jean-Cap-Ferrat

☎ 04 93 01 33 09

🌐 15 Feb–1 Nov 10–6 (till 7 Jul/Aug); 2 Nov–14 Feb 2–6 (weekdays), 10–6 (weekends and school hols)

🍴 Salon de thé and terrace (££)

🚌 Beaulieu-sur-Mer

ℹ 06230 St-Jean-Cap-Ferrat ☎ 04 93 76 08 90

♿ Few

✋ Moderate

🔄 Beaulieu-sur-Mer (➤ 50); Villefranche (➤ 90)

❓ Guided tours available. Gift shop

View of the villa from the Temple of Love

Baroness Béatrice Ephrussi de Rothschild's rose-pink, belle époque *palace, the Île de France, is considered the finest on the Riviera.*

The flamboyant Béatrice, Baroness Ephrussi de Rothschild (1864–1934) and daughter of the Bank of France's director, was a woman of seemingly unlimited wealth who had a passion for travel and fine art. She created her dream villa here in 1912, in the glorious style of the great palaces of the Italian Renaissance, set in immaculate gardens. It took seven years to build, on one of the most beautiful sites of the Riviera, with sea views on all sides. She named the villa after a memorable voyage on an ocean liner, the *Île de France*, and designed the main garden in the shape of a ship's deck with a Temple of Love on the bow. She even made her 35 gardeners dress as sailors.

The interior of the villa is lavishly decorated with rare furniture (including some pieces that once belonged to Marie Antoinette), set off by rich carpets, tapestries and an eclectic collection of rare *objets d'art*, and one of the world's most beautiful collections of Vincennes and Sèvres porcelain. Despite being filled with priceless works of art, the villa has retained the atmosphere of an occupied residence, as shown in a fascinating film that retraces the history of the house and evokes the daily life on the Riviera during the *belle epoque*.

The villa is surrounded by seven delightful theme gardens: Spanish, Florentine, lapidary, Japanese, exotic, Provençal and English.

What to See

How the locals relax – a game of boules

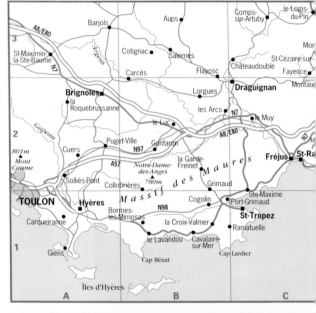

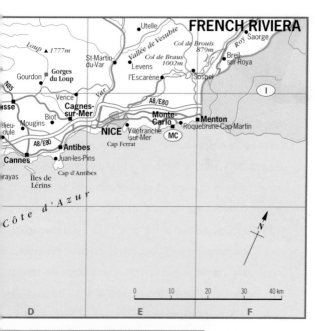

FRENCH RIVIERA

Utelle · Saorge
Loup ▲1777m
Vallée de Vesubie
St-Martin- *Col de Brouis*
du-Var *879m*
Gourdon **Gorges** *Col de Braus* Breil
du Loup Levens *1002m* sur-Roya
N85 l'Escarène · Sospel
sse
Vence *Var*
Biot **Cagnes-** A8/E80 I
lieu- Mougins **sur-Mer** **Monte-**
oule **Carlo** ■**Menton**
A8/E80 **NICE** Villefranche- Roquebrune-Cap-Martin
■**Cannes** ●**Antibes** -sur-Mer MC
rayas ●Juan-les-Pins Cap Ferrat
Îles de Cap d'Antibes
Lérins

Côte d'Azur

N

0   10   20   30   40 km

D   E   F

Seaside boulevards, palm trees, marinas and elegant café terraces are the hallmarks of a classic Riviera resort

Nice

'Queen of the Riviera', 'Capital of the Côte d'Azur', 'The Big Olive', 'Mediterranean Chicago', 'Nizza la Bella' – no accolade is too great for Nice, the Riviera's largest, most interesting city, France's main tourist centre and the country's most visited city after Paris. Yet despite its status, it remains a friendly, informal place, unscathed by tourism and full of Mediterranean character, with its own dialect (*lenga nissarda*), its own delicious cuisine – a seductive mix of the best of France and Italy – and an intriguing past. The city is lively all year round, offering exhibitions, shows, sporting events and festivals – in particular the famous Nice Carnival (two weeks before Lent) and the Battle of the Flowers. Come and experience Nice's original atmosphere for yourself. You are sure to be spellbound.

> *'If you would like to see the most beautiful land in the world, here it is'*
>
> PIERRE AUGUSTE RENOIR

●

Nice

This magnificent all-year-round resort, so agreeably named 'Nice', is a vibrant city, shaped by a colourful past. It offers visitors a fascinating blend of ancient and modern, innumerable attractions, a wonderful climate, and a carefree *joie de vivre*, as it sits beside the glittering Baie des Anges (Bay of Angels), basking in the scorching Mediterranean sun.

Nice was originally founded by the Greeks in the 4th century BC, followed by the Romans, who had a settlement at Cimiez (later ruined by Saracens). Nice thrived again in the Middle Ages, first under the Counts of Provence, then under the Italian Dukes of Savoy. Unified with France only as recently as 1860, it retains a strong Italianate character, admirably combining Italian temperament and lifestyle with French finesse and *savoir-faire*.

Bird's-eye view of the popular Baie des Anges at Nice

Thanks mainly to the English, Nice was already Europe's most fashionable winter retreat by the 1860s, with exuberant *belle époque* hotels springing up along the fashionable palm-lined waterfront, which is aptly named Promenade des Anglais. Near by, the narrow alleys and vibrant markets of the Vieille Ville (Old Town) contrast boldly with the broad boulevards and designer boutiques of the modern metropolis that fans out from place Masséna, Nice's handsome main square. The entire city is cradled by the impressive vine-clad foothills of the Alpes-Maritimes.

This delightful setting has attracted many artists over the years. As a result Nice is blessed with more museums and galleries than any French town outside Paris, and has been voted the city where French people would most like to live.

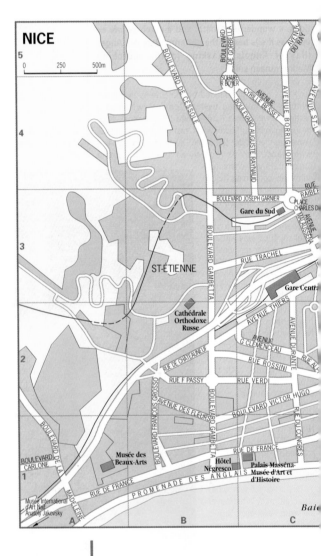

NICE

5

0   250   500m

BOULEVARD DE GORBELLA

AVENUE DU RAY

BOULEVARD DE CESSOLE

SQUARE
R BOYER

BOULEVARD AUGUSTE RAYNAUD

AVENUE CYRILLE BESSE

AVENUE BORRIGLIONE

AVENUE ST

4

RUE
RAIBEF

BOULEVARD JOSEPH GARNIER

Gare du Sud

PLACE
CHARLES D

BOULEVARD GAMBETTA

RUE TRACHEL

AVENUE
HAUSSM

3

ST-ETIENNE

Gare Centra

Cathédrale
Orthodoxe
Russe

AVENUE THIERS

AVENUE DURANTE

RUE AL

AVENUE
G CLEMENCEAU

RUE DE CHATEAUNEUF

RUE ROSSINI

2

RUE F PASSY

RUE VERDI

AVENUE DES FLEURS

BOULEVARD FRANCOIS GROSSO

BOULEVARD GAMBETTA

BOULEVARD VICTOR HUGO

RUE DU CONGRES

BOULEVARD DE LA

BOULEVARD
CARLONE

RUE DE FRANCE

Musée des
Beaux-Arts

Hôtel
Négresco

RUE DE FRANCE

Palais Masséna-
Musée d'Art et
d'Histoire

1

Musée International
d'Art Naïf
Anatoly Jakovsky

MADELEINE

RUE DE FRANCE

PROMENADE DES ANGLAIS

Baie

A

B

C

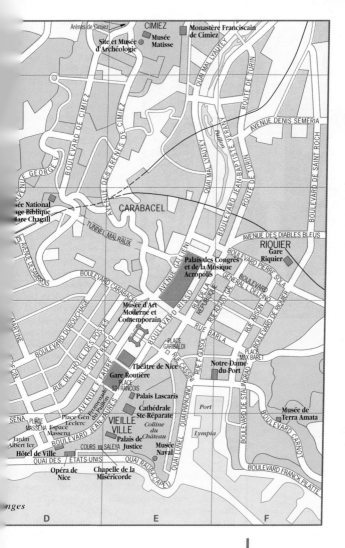

Arènes de Cimiez

CIMIEZ

Monastère Franciscain de Cimiez

Site et Musée d'Archéologie

Musée Matisse

BOULEVARD DE CIMIEZ

AVENUE DES ARÈNES DE CIMIEZ

QUAI MAL L'AUTEY

QUAI MAL L'AUTEY

AVENUE DENIS SÉMÉRIA

ROUTE DE TURIN

BOULEVARD JEAN-BAPTISTE VÉRANY

ROUTE DE TURIN

BOULEVARD DE SAINT ROCH

AVENUE GEORGE

AVENUE DESMBROIS

Musée National Message Biblique Marc Chagall

CARABACEL

TUNNEL MALRAUX

AVENUE DES DIABLES BLEUS

RIQUIER

Gare Riquier

Palais des Congrès et de la Musique Acropolis

BOULEVARD PIERRE SOLA

BOULEVARD CARABACEL

AVENUE GALLIENI

AVENUE RISSO

RUE DE LA RÉPUBLIQUE

GÉNÉRAL L DELFINO

BOULEVARD

BOULEVARD DE RIQUIER

RUE ARSON

BOULEVARD DU BOUCHAGE

RUE DE L'HÔTEL DES POSTES

RUE GIOFFREDO

Musée d'Art Moderne et Contemporain

BOULEVARD RISSO

RUE AUGUSTE GAL

RUE BARLA

MARTINE

BOULEVARD DUBOUCHAGE

RUE CASSINI

PLACE GARIBALDI

PLACE MAX BARET

RUE F GUISOL

CFIN

AVENUE JEAN MÉDECIN

AVENUE MALAUSSÉNA

Théâtre de Nice

Gare Routière

PLACE ST-FRANÇOIS

Palais Lascaris

RUE PAPACINO

Notre-Dame-du-Port

SÉNA

PLACE MASSÉNA

Espace Masséna

Place Gén Leclerc

Promenade du Paillon

BOULEVARD JEAN JAURÈS

Cathédrale Ste-Réparate

VIEILLE VILLE

Colline du Château

Port

QUAI LUNEL

BOULEVARD DE STALINGRAD

Musée de Terra Amata

BOULEVARD CARNOT

Jardin Albert Ier

Hôtel de Ville

Palais de Justice

COURS SALEYA

Musée Naval

Lympia

QUAI RAUBA-CAPEU

QUAI DES ÉTATS-UNIS

Opéra de Nice

Chapelle de la Miséricorde

BOULEVARD FRANCK PILATTE

nges

D

E

F

What to See in Nice

CATHÉDRALE ★ ORTHODOXE RUSSE

This magnificent pink and grey Russian Orthodox church, crowned by six gleaming green onion-shaped cupolas, was built by Tsar Nicolas II in 1903 in memory of his son Nicolas, who is buried in the grounds. The young, consumptive Tsarevich Nicolas was brought to Nice in search of good health in 1865, but to no avail. The luxurious villa in which he died was later demolished to construct the cathedral and a mortuary chapel.

The interior takes the form of a Greek cross and is brimming with precious icons, frescoes and treasures. The lavish iconostasis separating the sanctuary from the nave features a striking icon of Our Lady of Kazan, painted on wood and set amidst a riot of silver and precious stones. The church still conducts regular services in Russian.

CATHÉDRALE STE-RÉPARATE ★

Nice's beautiful baroque cathedral was built by local architect Jean-André Guibera in 1650 and dedicated to the city's patron saint, Réparate, who was martyred in Asia Minor at the tender age of 15.

The building is dominated by an 18th-century bell tower and a magnificent emerald dome of Niçoise tiles. The carefully proportioned façade, with its arcaded entrance, decorative niches and medallions, dates from 1825 and has recently been enhanced with colour.

Inside, visitors are confronted by a profusion of baroque marble, stucco and gilt. Note the ornate marble high altar and choir balustrade, the walnut panelling in the sacristy, acquired from Nice's Dominican convent, and the painting *Dispute du Saint-Sacrement* in the right transept, attributed to the Raphaël School.

✚ 32B2
✉ avenue Nicolas II
🕐 9:30–12, 2:30–5. Closed Sun AM
❓ No shorts or sleeveless shirts

✚ 33E2
✉ place Rossetti
🚌 All buses
♿ Good
🖐 Free
❓ No shorts or sleeveless shirts

Above: the exotic domes of the Russian Orthodox church evoke Nice's cosmopolitan heyday

CIMIEZ ✪✪✪

Cimiez is a district of luxury villas and palatial residences on the low hills overlooking the city. A monument dedicated to Queen Victoria outside her favourite winter residence, the recently renovated Hôtel Regina, serves as a reminder that Cimiez was frequently visited by royalty at the turn of the century. It is still considered to be Nice's smartest residential quarter.

As early as 140 BC, the Romans built a town on the hills of Cimiez called Cemenelum which, by the end of the 2nd century AD, had 20,000 inhabitants and was the capital of the Roman Alpes Maritimae province. The remains of a small amphitheatre (Arènes), paved streets and public baths have been excavated at the top of the Boulevard de Cimiez. A small, modern museum (Musée d'Archéologie) displays the finds and illustrates the city's history from the Bronze Age to medieval times.

Near by is the Musée Matisse (➤ 23). Both museums back on to an old olive grove that is the venue for Europe's leading international Jazz Festival in July, attracting top celebrities from all over the world. At the eastern end of the grove is the **Monastère Franciscain de Cimiez** (Franciscan Monastery) and the church of Notre-Dame-de-l'Assomption.

The Franciscans have used the church and monastery since 1546. Inside are two masterpieces by Louis Bréa, a leading painter of the Nice School, and an impressive carved altarpiece. A museum in the monastic buildings evokes the life of Franciscan monks in Nice from the 13th to the 18th centuries. Dufy and Matisse lie buried in the adjacent cemetery overlooking Nice.

Site et Musée d'Archéologie

🚩 33E5
✉ 160 avenue des Arènes
☎ 04 93 81 59 57
🕐 Apr–Sep 10–12, 2–6;
Oct–Mar 10–1, 2–5.
Closed Mon and some
hols
🚌 15, 17, 20, 22, 25
♿ Few
💷 Expensive
❓ Guided tours 1st Wed of
month at 3PM

Monastère Franciscain de Cimiez

🚩 33E5
✉ place du Monastère
☎ 04 93 81 00 04
🕐 10–12, 3–6. Closed Sun
and hols
🚌 15, 17, 20, 22, 25
♿ Few
💷 Free
❓ Guided tours Mon–Fri
10:30, 3:30, 4:30

Above: *stylish
art-deco villas dot
the Cimiez dstrict*

35

➕ 33E1
✉ Colline du Château
☎ 04 93 85 62 33
🕐 Mon–Sat 10–5:30
🍴 Café (£)
🚌 38
♿ Few
🎟 Free

Musée Naval

➕ 33E1
✉ Colline du Château
☎ 04 93 80 47 61
🕐 Wed–Sun 10–12, 2–5, until 7 in summer. Closed Mon, Tue and mid-Nov to mid-Dec
♿ Few

➕ 33D1
✉ cours Saleya
🕐 Fruit and vegetable market: Tue–Sun 6AM–1PM. Flower market: all day except Sun PM; Flea market: Mon AM
🚌 All buses

The Cours Saleya, with its vibrant cafés and stuccoed buildings, has a distinctly Italianate air

COLLINE DU CHÂTEAU (CASTLE HILL) ✪✪

Surprisingly, there is no château here. The city's fortress was destroyed by the French in the early 18th century when Nice belonged to Savoy. Instead, you will find cool, shady gardens with absorbing views over the crowded old port (Quartier du Port ➤ 43), the gleaming, glazed tiles of the old town (Vieille Ville ➤ 44) and the voluptuous curve of the Baie des Anges.

It was on this imposing site that Nice originated as the ancient Greek acropolis of Nikaïa. Archaeologists have since discovered Roman and medieval remains, some of which have been housed in a tiny lapidary museum on the hill.

The best approach is up the steps on quai des Etats-Unis, or by lift from nearby Tour Bellanda, which also houses the small **Naval Museum**. Descend eastwards along montée Eberlé and rue Catherine Ségurane to the elegant, arcaded place Garibaldi, which is named after the great Niçoise revolutionary Giuseppe Garibaldi (hero of Italy's unification) who lies buried in a cemetery at the top of the hill.

COURS SALEYA ✪✪✪

Every morning (except Monday, which is reserved for antique dealers), this spacious, sunny square is the scene of one of France's best fruit, flower and vegetable markets. The colourful stands overflow with locally grown produce, including flowers, olives, honey, tomatoes, aubergines, citrus fruits and *herbes de Provence* – the tastes, fragrances and colours of Provence and Italy are a veritable feast for the senses.

Arrive at dawn and you will find the Riviera's top chefs choosing their *plats du jour* from the tempting food displays. During the day, it is fun to watch the world go by from the pavement terraces of the countless bars and

restaurants that line the famous market, or to try a light snack from the market stalls. Look out for *pissaladière* (onion tart with anchovy and olives), *beignets de courgettes* (frittered courgette flowers) or visit Madame Thérèse's stall for the best *socca* (traditional Niçoise chickpea pancake) in town. At night, cafés and restaurants come into their own, making this one of Nice's most animated nightspots.

Surely one of the world's most famous hotels

Did you know ?

Isadora Duncan, the infamous American dancer, spent her last months in the Hôtel Négresco, until her untimely death outside the hotel in 1927, when her trailing scarf caught in the wheel of her Bugatti and broke her neck.

HÔTEL NÉGRESCO ⭐⭐

Churchill, Chaplin, Piaf, Picasso, Taylor and Burton, the Beatles… The Négresco's guest list is legendary. It was built in 1912 for Henri Négresco, once a gypsy-violin serenader, who went bankrupt eight years later. Nevertheless, it remains a famous Riviera landmark, a National Historic Monument and one of France's most magnificent hotels.

The interior is full of surprises, ranging from the world's largest Aubusson carpet to gaudy, gold glittery bathroom suites. The décor is inspired by Versailles and the lavatories are more lavishly ornamented than many other hotel lounges.

From the outside, its pink-and-white turreted façade looks more like a wedding cake than a hotel. You may have trouble finding the main entrance because it is in a small back street. The whole hotel was built backwards to protect guests from the then unfashionable sun!

- 🚩 32B1
- ✉ 37 promenade des Anglais
- ☎ 04 93 16 64 00
- 🍴 Le Chantecler (£££) (► 93); La Rotonde (£) (► 92)
- 🚌 6, 7, 9, 10, 12, airport bus
- ♿ Very good
- ↔ Musée des Beaux-Arts (► 38); Palais Masséna (► 40)

Carle van Loo's great Neptune et Amymone *(1757)*

MAMAC (► 22, TOP TEN)

MUSÉE DES BEAUX-ARTS ⭐⭐

Once home to a Ukranian princess, this handsome residence, built in the style of 17th-century Genoese palaces, is now home to Nice's Museum of Fine Art.

The collection began with a donation from Napoléon II and includes works from 17th-century Italian Old Masters right through to contemporary works. One entire gallery is given over to 18th-century Niçoise artist Carle Van Loo (1705–65) and the main staircase is adorned with the works of Jules Chéret (1836–1932), a popular *belle époque* lithographist, who introduced colour advertising posters to France in 1866.

The École Française is also well represented, with works by Dégas, Boudin and Sisley. Sculptures by Rodin and Carpeaux also form part of the collection, together with important impressionist and post-impressionist works by Bonnard, Vuillard and Van Dongen (including his famous *Tango of the Archangel* – an entertaining evocation of the roaring twenties on the Riviera).

The main attraction of the museum is an exceptional collection of works by the impressionist café-society artist, Raoul Dufy, recently moved from the Musée Dufy on the waterfront because the salt air was affecting the paint. Of particular note are the early fauve works, the 1908 *Bâteaux à l'Estaque* (a cubist painting predating cubism), and a handful of colourful Nice scenes.

MUSÉE INTERNATIONAL D'ART NAÏF ANATOLY JAKOVSKY ⭐

The International Museum of Naïve Art is housed in an elegant, turn-of-the-century pink villa, the Château de Ste-Hélène, built by the perfume magnate, Coty.

It contains a remarkable 600 canvases, drawings, engravings and sculptures, donated by Anatoly Jakovsky, illustrating the history of naïve art throughout the world from the 17th century to the present day. Croatian artists

Sidebar (Musée des Beaux-Arts):

✚ 32A1
✉ 33 avenue des Baumettes
☎ 04 93 44 50 72
🕐 10–12, 2–6. Closed Mon and some hols
🚌 3, 6, 7, 9, 10, 12, 14, 22
♿ Good
🎫 Moderate

Sidebar (Musée International d'Art Naïf):

✚ 32A1
✉ Château Ste-Hélène, avenue du Val Marie
☎ 04 93 71 78 33
🕐 10–12, 2–6. Closed Tue and some hols
🚌 6, 9, 10, 12, 23, 24, 26, 34
♿ Few 🎫 Expensive

are especially well represented, including Generalič, Kovačić and Petrović. Look out also for French masters of the genre, including Vivin, Rimbert and Bauchant.

MUSÉE MATISSE (► 23, TOP TEN)

MUSÉE NATIONAL ✪✪✪
MESSAGE BIBLIQUE MARC CHAGALL

Located in the heart of a Mediterranean garden at the foot of Cimiez hill (► 35), this striking, modern museum was especially designed by André Hermant to exhibit Marc Chagall's 'Biblical Message' – a series of 17 monumental canvases, created between 1954 and 1967, evoking the Garden of Eden, Moses and other biblical themes.

Chagall was a highly individualistic Russian-Jewish painter who drew his main themes from the Old Testament and Russian-Jewish folklore. Born in Vitebsk in 1887, he spent the war years in America, before moving permanently to St-Paul-de-Vence in 1950.

He opened the museum here himself in 1973. He also created the mosaic of the prophet Elijah, cleverly reflected in the pool, and the beautiful blue stained-glass windows representing *The Creation of the World* in the concert hall. Other works were donated to the museum after Chagall's death in 1985, making this the largest and most important permanent collection of his work.

🔢 33D3
✉ avenue Docteur Ménard
☎ 04 93 53 87 20
🕐 Jul–Sep 10–6; Oct–Jun 10–5. Closed Tue, 1 Jan, 1 May, 25 Dec
🍴 Garden café, Apr–Oct (£)
🚌 15
♿ Excellent
💷 Very expensive
🔁 Cimiez (► 35); Musée Matisse (► 23)
❓ Shop, library, concert hall. Reserve guided tours in advance

Visitors marvel at Chagall's distinctive works

PALAIS LASCARIS ✪

33E2

✉ 15 rue Droite

☎ 04 93 62 05 54

🕐 10–12, 2:30–6. Closed Mon and some hols

🚌 1, 2, 3, 5, 6, 14, 16, 17, 25, 37

♿ Few

💳 Moderate

In a narrow back street at the heart of the Vieille Ville, behind a façade of ornate balconies and pilasters adorned with garlands of flowers, lies the beautiful Palais Lascaris. This Genoese-style palace was originally four separate houses, bought in 1648 by the powerful Lascaris-Ventimiglia family. The city of Nice purchased the property in 1942 and has since restored this noble building.

In the entrance hall the family coat of arms is engraved on the ceiling, bearing the motto 'Not even lightning strikes us'. On the ground floor there is a reconstruction of a pharmacy dated 1738, with an unusual collection of porcelain vases. A grandiose balustraded staircase, decorated with 17th-century paintings and statues of Mars and Venus, leads to sumptuous reception rooms containing elegant chandeliers, Flemish tapestries, 17th- and 18th-century furniture, ornate woodwork and a trompe-l'oeil ceiling.

PALAIS MASSÉNA – MUSÉE D'ART ET D'HISTOIRE ✪

32C1

✉ 35 promenade des Anglais and 65 rue de France

☎ 04 93 88 06 22

🕐 10–12, 2–6 (Oct–Mar 2–5). Closed Mon and some hols

🚌 3, 6, 7, 9, 10, 12, 14, 22

♿ Few

💳 Moderate

Palais Masséna was built in the first Empire style in 1901 by Prince Victor Masséna, the great-grandson of Nice-born Marshal Masséna, Napoléon's ruthlessly ambitious military genius. The building was bequeathed to the city of Nice on the condition that it become a museum devoted to regional history.

The solemn statue of Napoléon that stands near the entrance sets the tone for the wide-ranging historical exhibits inside, which include paintings by members of the early Nice School, a library containing over 10,000 rare books and manuscripts, and a fearsome collection of 15th- and 16th-century weaponry. There are various rooms dedicated to Garibaldi, Napoléon, Marshal Masséna and the Nice plebiscite of 1860. A fascinating section is reserved for local traditions; especially enjoyable are the collections of costumes, furniture, faïence pottery and regional craftwork.

Handsome Prince Masséna still guards his palace

Gardens and Promenades

Start at the Acropolis (➤ 43). Head southwards, climbing up a flight of steps to MAMAC (➤ 22) and the Théâtre de Nice.

The monumental, marble-clad Museum of Modern Art (MAMAC) and the 282-million-franc Théâtre de Nice (TDN) are Nice's answer to Paris' Pompidou Centre.

Continue beyond the theatre into the gardens of the promenade du Paillon, climbing to the highest level.

These 'hanging gardens' cleverly hide a hideous concrete car park and the ugly main bus station below. Although a pleasant place to stroll by day, this area is best avoided after dusk.

Go down the steps (to the right of the car park) and cross the road into place Général Leclerc. Continue across allée Résistance et Déportation, through espace Masséna and on to place Masséna (➤ 42).

Espace Masséna, lined with benches and with fountains that bubble both day and night, is a popular yet peaceful place to cool off in the summer. By contrast, neighbouring place Masséna is one of Nice's busiest squares.

More gardens (Jardins Albert I) lead to the waterfront. Turn right on to the Promenade des Anglais (➤ 42).

The Promenade des Anglais follows the gracious curve of the Baie des Anges, past *belle époque* mansions and follies created by English lords and Russian aristocrats in Nice's heyday. In summer there is a small open-air theatre (Théâtre de Verdure) in the gardens.

Continue along the waterfront until you reach Hôtel Négresco.

Distance
2.5km

Time
1–1½ hours

Start point
Acropolis
✚ 33E3
🚌 all buses

End point
Hôtel Négresco
✚ 32C1
🚌 6, 7, 9, 10, 12, airport bus

Lunch
La Rotonde (££) (➤ 93)
✉ Hôtel Négresco, 37 promenade des Anglais
☎ 04 93 16 64 00

France's favourite pet takes 'Madame' for a walk

+ 32B1

✉ promenade des Anglais

🚌 3, 6, 7, 9, 10, 12, 14, 22, 23, 24, 26, 34, airport bus

♿ Very good

↔ Musée des Beaux-Arts (➤ 38); Musée International d'Art Naïf (➤ 38)

? Casino ☎ 04 93 87 95 87; open-air theatre in Jardin Albert Iᵉʳ ☎ 04 92 17 40 40

Above: *a welcome breeze on the Promenade des Anglais*

+ 33E3

PROMENADE DES ANGLAIS ●●●

The Promenade des Anglais is one of Nice's great trademarks. As its name suggests, this palm-lined promenade, which stretches along the curvaceous Baie des Anges (Bay of Angels), was constructed at the expense of Nice's wealthy English residents in 1822, so that they could stroll along the shoreline.

Originally the promenade was a simple coastal path only 2m wide. Today it is a frenetic highway of *autoroute* porportions and the white wedding-cake style architecture of the luxury *belle époque* hotels, such as the world famous Négresco (➤ 37) are now juxtaposed with ugly concrete apartment blocks.

The Promenade des Anglais backs a 6km stretch of pebble beaches, washed by a brilliant azure sea. To the north lies a cobweb of busy pedestrianised streets, brimming with restaurants, bars and chic boutiques.

QUARTIER DU PAILLON ●●

The once fast-flowing and often dangerously high River Paillon was canalised in the 1830s and began to vanish under the pavements. It now trickles below Nice's showcase gardens – lush Jardins Albert Iᵉʳ, fountain-filled éspace Masséna, leafy place Général Leclerc and the

Did you know ?

The Bay of Angels took its celestial name from the story of Réparate, Nice's 15-year-old patron saint, who died a martyr in Caesarea in Palestine. One evening in the year AD 250, fishermen in the bay saw a frail boat containing the young girl asleep on a bed of flowers, guided by two angels and a dove, bringing Réparate home to Nice.

delightful hanging gardens of the promenade du Paillon (▶ 41).

The Paillon district's main focal point is place Masséna, a stately 19th-century square featuring red-ochre buildings built across the path of the river. Many important streets fan out from the square, notably avenue Jean Médecin (Nice's main shopping street) and rue Masséna (a lively pedestrian zone). A balustraded terrace and steps to the south lead to the old town (Vieille Ville ▶ 44). To the north the covered course of the river provided space for several grand civic projects built during the last 20 years: a row of cultural complexes including the state-of-the-art MAMAC building (▶ 22), the **Théâtre de Nice** and the **Acropolis** convention centre, a monumental eyesore of concrete slabs and smoked glass.

QUARTIER DU PORT ✪✪

For centuries there was no port at Nice. Local boats simply moored in the lee of the castle rock while larger ships anchored in Villefranche Harbour. It was only in 1750 that Charles-Emmanuel III, Duke of Savoy, saw the potential trading benefits, and excavated a deep-water port at the mouth of the Lympia River.

Today Lympia port is busy with craft of all kinds, from tiny traditional fishing barques to car ferries from Corsica. It is flanked by striking red-ochre, 18th-century buildings and the neo-classical church of Notre-Dame-du-Port. It is best approached via a windy headland, aptly named quai Rauba-Capéu ('hat-thief'), past a colossal monument commemorating the 4,000 Niçoise who died during World War I. On a hill to the east, the **Musée de Terra Amata**, built on the site of an excavated fossil beach, documents prehistoric life in the region.

A yachtsman's view of Nice from the old port

Théâtre de Nice
- 🏛 33E2
- ✉ promenade des Arts
- ☎ 04 93 80 52 60
- 🕐 1–7PM. Closed Sun and Mon
- 🍴 Café and restaurant (£-££)
- 🚌 All buses

Acropolis
- 🏛 33E3
- ✉ 1 esplanade Kennedy
- ☎ 04 93 92 83 00
- 🚌 4, 5, 6, 15, 16, 17, 35
- ♿ Excellent
- ↔ Cimiez (▶ 35); MAMAC (▶ 22); Musée National Marc Chagall (▶ 39)

Musée de Terra Amata
- 🏛 33F1
- ✉ 25 boulevard Carnot
- ☎ 04 93 55 59 93
- 🕐 Tue–Sun 9–12, 2–6. Closed Mon
- 🚌 1, 2, 7, 9, 14, 20, 32
- ♿ Few
- 💷 Expensive

The charming, narrow streets of Vieux Nice beckon...

Galerie de Malacologie
- ⊠ 3 cours Saleya
- ☎ 04 93 85 18 44
- 🕐 Dec–Oct, Tue–Sat 10:30–1, 2–6 (6:30 from May–Sep). Closed Sun, Mon and hols
- 🚌 All buses
- ♿ Few
- 👋 Moderate

Galerie des Ponchettes
- ⊠ 77 quai des Etats-Unis
- ☎ 04 93 62 31 24
- 🕐 Tue–Sat 10–12, 2–6. Sun 2–6. Closed Mon and hols
- 🚌 All buses
- ♿ Good
- 👋 Moderate

Galerie-Musée Mossa
- ⊠ 59 quai des Etats-Unis
- ☎ 04 93 62 37 11
- 🕐 Tue–Sat 10–12, 2–6. Sun 2–6. Closed Mon and hols
- 🚌 All buses
- ♿ Good
- 👋 Moderate

VIEILLE VILLE ✪✪✪

The best way to discover Nice is to get lost in the tangle of dark, narrow streets of the Vieille Ville (Old Town), festooned with flowers and laundry and brimming with cafés, hidden squares and bustling markets. Dismissed as a dangerous slum in the 1970s, this is now the trendiest and most scenic part of Nice, with its stylish Italianate buildings painted in sunny terracotta reds with cool green shutters.

In the back streets, designer boutiques, atmospheric galleries and intimate Nissart restaurants rub shoulders with no-nonsense workers' cafés and run-of-the-mill stores catering for the daily needs of the locals. The rue du Marché, rue de la Boucherie, rue du Collet and rue Pairolière have the atmosphere of a covered market, lined with photogenic food stalls. For early risers, a visit to the pungent fish market on place St-François is an interesting and rewarding experience.

The old town's heart beats loudest at the Cours Saleya (► 36). Lively both day and night, with its enticing daily market, alfresco restaurants, cafés and clubs, it also contains some striking architecture, including the Église de l'Annonciation, one of the oldest churches in Nice, and the Chapelle de la Miséricorde, with its Piedmontese baroque façade and flamboyant rococo interior.

Near by are several quirky museums including a tiny shell gallery – **Galerie de Malacologie** – **Galerie des Ponchettes,** showing temporary art exhibitions, and **Galerie-Musée Mossa.** Alexis Mossa reinitiated the famous Nice Carnival and painted it in watercolours, while his son Gustav produced lurid symbolist paintings.

A Walk around the Vieille Ville

Start at the western end of the Cours Saleya.

This square is where Nice's famous outdoor flower, fruit and vegetable market is held (➤ 36), an ideal place to hear the local patois and to taste local Nissart delicacies.

Head east past the palace of the former Dukes of Savoy and the Italianate 18th-century Chapelle de la Misericorde to the yellow house at the end of the square, where Matisse once lived. Turn left into rue Gilly, then continue along rue Droite, past Palais Lascaris (➤ 40).

Tempting bars and brasseries line the market square

Rue Droite contains some of the old town's top galleries and Provence's best bread shop, Espuno (➤ 109).

Continue straight on as far as place St-François and the early morning fish market.

Unusually, this is an inland fish market but, before the River Paillon was filled in, fishermen used to land here to sell their catch.

Continue down rue St-François. Bear right into rue du Collet, left at place Centrale along rue Centrale, then right into rue Mascoïnat until you reach place Rossetti.

Place Rossetti is dominated by the beautiful baroque Cathédrale Ste-Réparate (➤ 34), with its emerald dome of Niçoise tiles. Enjoy a coffee in one of the cafés here or an ice-cream from Fenocchio's (➤ 93).

Leave the square along rue Ste-Réparate. At the end, turn right into rue de la Préfecture.

The great violinist Niccolò Paganini lived and died at No 23.

A right turn opposite Paganini's house into rue St-Gaètan takes you back to the Cours Saleya.

Distance
2km

Time
1–2 hours, depending on shopping, museum and church visits

Start/end point
Cours Saleya
🚇 33D1
🚌 All buses

Lunch
La Criée (££) (➤ 92)
✉ 22 cours Saleya
☎ 04 93 85 49 99

The Riviera

The resorts of this incredible stretch of coastline, surveyed from afar by snow-capped mountains, have virtually fused together into one giant, bustling megalopolis. The original piece of coast to which the name 'Riviera' was applied, when it began to be fashionable as a winter resort in the 19th century, was the stretch between Menton and Nice – which still evoke their *belle époque* grandeur. Now the term is taken to include the fashionable yacht-havens of Antibes and Cannes, and a string of popular family resorts stretching as far as trend-setting St-Tropez.

Yet behind this glamorous coastline lies the authentic soul of the region: a picturesque landscape of vineyards, olive groves and fields of lavender, dotted with ancient, fragrant honey-coloured villages. Here the pace of life is slow and villagers play *boules* in the shade of plane trees or laze in cafés, gazing out to the distant Côte d'Azur.

> *'In short, I think life here is a happier thing than in countless other spots on earth'*
>
> VINCENT VAN GOGH

———————●———————

Villefranche Harbour has a long history – its deep waters sheltered galleys in Roman times

*Explore the cool, shady
alleys of Antibes*

ANTIBES ✪✪

Antibes was founded in the 5th century BC as a Greek
trading post called Antipolis ('the city opposite'),
presumably because of its location opposite Nice, or
Nikaïa. The two cities later became true opposites, with
Antibes as the frontier town of France whilst Nice was
controlled by the Dukes of Savoy until the 18th century.
Hence Vauban's mighty 17th-century Fort Carré on the
eastern edge of the town, where Napoléon was once held
prisoner, and the massive ancient ramparts, which today
protect the old town of Antibes from flooding.

Tucked just behind the ramparts is Vieux Antibes (Old
Antibes), a honey-coloured quarter of winding, cobbled
lanes, splashed with flowers and overflowing with shops,
restaurants and bars. Be sure to visit the bustling morning
market in the cours
Masséna, and the craft
market which takes place
Friday and Sunday after-
noons (also Tuesday and
Thursday in summer).

Alongside the market
stands a 12th- to 16th-
century seafront château,
the former seat of the
Grimaldi family, that today
houses one of the world's
finest Picasso collections
(➤ 25). Beside the castle,
the bold red and yellow
Église de l'Immaculée
Conception represents a
hotchpotch of periods and
styles. Its 11th-century
belfry was formerly the
town's main watchtower.

On the waterfront, the
Port Vauban Yacht Harbour
boasts some of the
Riviera's most luxurious
yachts. Near by, the Cap
d'Antibes promontory was
the first coastal resort to
welcome rich tourists in
the mid-19th century. Its
beach is still considered by
many the best place to
enjoy the sun.

A Circular Drive from Antibes

Leave Antibes on the N7 following signs to Cannes and Golfe-Juan. After a while, Vallauris is signposted. Drive through Golfe-Juan and up the D135 to Vallauris.

Vallauris is one of Provence's main pottery centres, made famous by Picasso, who lived here between 1946 and 1955. With over 200 potters working here, the town's streets are crammed with touristy ceramics shops, but the Musée Municipal and the Musée National Picasso (in a deconsecrated chapel) are worth a visit.

Continue up the D135 towards Grasse. Cross over the autoroute past Mougins' Musée de l'Automobile (➤ 112) and through a forest (Parc Forestier Départemental de la Valmasque). Turn left at the T-junction on to the D35 to Mougins.

Mougins is one of the Riviera's smartest villages, brimming with renowned restaurants (➤ 76).

Leave Mougins following signs to Mouans-Sartoux.

Mouans-Sartoux is designed on a grid pattern with the residential streets running north to south and the commercial streets east to west. Its main attraction is the 19th-century château, which houses an unusual permanent exhibition of concrete art.

Continue on the D85 to Grasse. Leave Grasse on the D2085 (direction Nice). After 6km, take the first exit (D3) to Valbonne.

This charming village fans out from the place des Arcades, a beautiful arcaded square and scene of an annual olive and grape festival in February, and an ideal venue for coffee or lunch (➤ 98).

From Valbonne, take the D4 to Biot (➤ 50) then return to Antibes on the D4 and the N7.

Distance
66km

Time
1½ hours; full day with visits

Start/end point
Antibes
✚ 57C2

Lunch
Auberge Provençale, Valbonne (£)
✉ place des Arcades
☎ 04 93 12 29 73

Biot is famous for its glass-blowing, especially its unique verre bullé (bubble glass)

49

72B2

place Clemenceau
☎ 04 93 01 02 21

Villa Kérylos

✉ impasse Eiffel
☎ 04 93 01 01 44
🕐 15 Mar–1 Nov daily
10:30–12:30, 2–6;
Jul–Aug 10–7; Sep 10–6;
1 Dec–14 Mar Tue–Fri
2–5:30, Sat–Sun
10:30–12:30, 2–5:30.
Closed Nov, 25 Dec and
1 Jan
♿ Few
💰 Expensive

57C3

place de la Chapelle
☎ 04 93 65 05 85
↔ Antibes (► 48), Cagnes
(► 52)

**Musée d'Histoire Locale et
de Céramique Biotoise**

✉ place de la Chapelle
☎ 04 93 65 11 79
🕐 Thu–Sun 2:30–6:30
♿ Few
💰 Moderate

Above: *one of many
potteries that Biot is
famous for*

BEAULIEU-SUR-MER ✪

Beaulieu really is a 'beautiful place' and one of the warmest resorts on the Riviera, sheltered by a natural amphitheatre of hills. It had its heyday at the turn of the century when many celebrities stayed here, including the Prince of Wales, Empress Sissi of Austria, Piotr Ilyich Tchaikovsky and Gustav Eiffel. It still boasts many attractions, including an elegant palm-lined promenade, a glamorous casino, the elegant Edwardian Rotonde and the extraordinary Villa Kérylos.

This seaside villa was built by archaeologist Théodore Reinach in 1908 as a tribute to life in ancient Greece. No expense was spared in its lavish décor of white, yellow and lavender marble, ivory and bronze. Reinach lived here for almost 20 years, eating, dressing and behaving as an Athenian citizen.

BIOT ✪✪✪

The pretty hilltop village of Biot is set in a typical Provençal landscape of cypresses, olives and pines, encompassing a mass of steep, cobbled lanes fanning out from the arcaded main square, lined by quaint sand-coloured houses with orange-tiled roofs and dotted with cafés and interesting antique shops.

Some of the streets are decorated with huge earthenware jars, ablaze with geraniums and tropical plants; for centuries, Biot has been a prosperous pottery centre. It is also known for its gold and silverwork, ceramics, olive wood carvings and thriving glassworks. The craftsmen's wares can be admired in the Musée d'Histoire Locale et de Céramique Biotoise while, at the Verrerie de Biot (► 105), visitors can watch glass-blowers demonstrating their unique *verre bullé* (bubble glass).

Twenty minutes' stroll from the old village is the **Musée Fernand Léger**, with a brilliantly coloured mosaic façade and huge stained-glass windows. The cubist painter Léger bought a villa here in 1955, intending to make Biot his home, but sadly died 15 days later. His widow founded the museum in 1959. It contains nearly 400 of his works, and was the first major museum in France to be dedicated entirely to one artist.

Musée Fernand Léger
- 04 92 91 50 30
- 10–12:30, 2–8 (winter 5:30). Closed Tue
- Good
- Expensive

BORMES-LES-MIMOSAS ✪✪

The village of Bormes, with its ice-cream coloured houses, is undoubtedly one of the Riviera's most picturesque villages. It has had a chequered history – founded by the Gauls, conquered by the Romans, then continually sacked by Saracens, Corsairs, Moors, Genoese and finally during the Wars of Religion. Depending on the season, it is bathed in the scent of mimosa, eucalyptus or camomile.

- 65A2
- 9 place Gambetta
- 04 94 71 15 17
- Collobrières (➤ 64), Massif des Maures (➤ 64)

Pause awhile in Bormes' sunny squares

During February, when the mimosa is in full bloom, the village celebrates with a sensational *corso fleuri* – an extravaganza of floral floats made from thousands of tiny yellow flowers.

A *circuit touristique* (tourist itinerary) spirals down steep stairways and alleys, with amusing names – *Venelle des Amoureux* (Lovers' Lane), *Draille des Bredouilles* (Gossipers' Way) and steepest of all, *rue Roumpi-Cuou* (Bottom-Breaker road)! On the way, it embraces most of the main sights, which include a fine 16th-century chapel dedicated to Bormes' patron saint, Saint François de Paule (who rescued the village from the plague in 1481), an 18th-century church built in Romanesque style, countless craft shops, and a ruined castle with dazzling views across the bay of le Lavandou and the Massif des Maures (➤ 64).

57C3

6 boulevard Maréchal
Juin ☎ 04 93 20 61 64

Biot (➤ 50), St-Paul-de-
Vence (➤ 78)

Château-Musée de Cagnes

✉ place Grimaldi, Haut-du-
Cagnes

☎ 04 93 20 85 57

🕐 Wed–Mon

♿ Few

💰 Cheap

Musée Renoir

✉ 19 chemin des Collettes

☎ 04 93 20 61 07

🕐 May–Oct 10–12, 2–6;
Dec–Apr 10–12, 2–5.
Closed Tue and Nov

♿ Few

💰 Moderate

Brightly coloured pointus
decorate Cros-de-Cagnes

CAGNES-SUR-MER ✪✪✪

Cagnes is divided into three: the main beach area and old
fishing quarter of Cros-de-Cagnes with its traditional boats
called *pointus* and a glut of excellent fish restaurants;
Cagnes-Ville, a busy commercial centre with a smart
racecourse (France's second largest) right beside the sea;
and Haut-de-Cagnes. This inviting hilltop village, with its
brightly coloured houses smothered in bougainvillaea,
mimosa and geraniums, is encircled by medieval ramparts
and crowned by a 14th-century castle, built as a pirate
lookout by Admiral Rainier Grimaldi. The castle contains
the **Château-Musée,** which houses several permanent
exhibitions, including the Olive Tree Museum and the
Museum of Modern Mediterranean Art, with works by
Chagall, Matisse and Renoir, Cagnes' most famous artist.

Pierre-Auguste Renoir spent the last 12 years of his life
just outside Cagnes at Domaine des Collettes, as
rheumatoid arthritis had forced him to leave Paris for a
slightly warmer climate. He chose Cagnes and, amongst
some 1,000-year-old olive trees, he built his villa, today
known as **Musée Renoir**. In the warm Mediterranean
sunshine, his work took on a new lease of life. Every day
he would sit at his easel for hours on end, his paintbrush
strapped to his rheumatic fingers. His palette, wheelchair
and other mementoes have been preserved, together with
several of his paintings, drawings, sculptures and bronzes;
the museum also contains works by other artists such as
Maillol, Bonnard and Dufy.

CANNES ⭐⭐

Think Cannes, think movies and film stars, expensive boutiques, palatial hotels and paparazzi. After all, it is one of the world's most chic resorts – the 'Queen of the coast', 'Pearl of the Riviera' – twinned with Beverly Hills and, within France, second only to Paris for shopping and major international cultural and business events, including the world-famous Cannes International Film Festival.

With so much glitz and glamour, it is easy to forget Cannes' humble origins as a simple fishing village, named after the canes and reeds of the surrounding marshes, since transformed into luxury yacht havens. Cannes was first put on the map in 1834 by retired British Chancellor Lord Brougham, who was forced to stop in Cannes en route to Nice. Enchanted by its warm climate and quaint setting, he abandoned his former plans, built a villa here and stayed for 34 winters, singing the praises of Cannes to his most distinguished compatriots! Shortly afterwards hundreds of gentry and royals followed his example. Grand hotels began to spring up along the waterfront and by the end of the century Cannes had become the 'aristocracy's winter lounge'.

In the 1920s, Cannes adopted a rhyme: 'Menton's dowdy, Monte's brass, Nice is rowdy, Cannes is class!'. However, it was not until the 1930s that Cannes became a summer resort, made fashionable by visiting Americans, including Harpo Marx and Scott and Zelda Fitzgerald, who used to frequent the gaming tables of Casino Croisette.

🔲 57B1

ℹ️ Palais des Festivals, 1 la Croisette ☎ 04 93 99 19 77

↔️ Îles de Lérins (➤ 21); Mandelieu/la Napoule (➤ 63); Mougins (➤ 76)

❓ Marché Forville: daily morning market (closed Mon in summer, Mon–Tue in winter)

Attentive service in the street cafés of Cannes

53

Above: *one of the great landmarks of la Croisette*

Opposite: *modern art on la Croisette typifies the glitter and glamour of Cannes*

Musée de la Castre

- ✉ Château de la Castre, le Suquet
- ☎ 04 93 38 55 26
- 🕐 Wed–Mon, Oct–Jun 10–12, 2–5; Jul–Sep 10–12, 2–6:30. Closed Tue and hols
- ♿ Few
- 🎟 Moderate

Palais des Festivals et des Congrès

- ✉ 1 la Croisette
- ☎ 04 93 39 24 53
- 🚌 8
- ❓ International Film Festival in May

By the 1950s mass summer tourism had taken off and it has been the life-blood of Cannes ever since.

Admittedly Cannes lacks the great museums, galleries and monuments of other large resorts or towns, but there is always plenty to do, with its casinos, fairs, beaches, boat trips to the Îles de Lérins (➤ 21), and its luxury boutiques, which flank the waterfront and the main shopping street, rue d'Antibes.

The town is divided into two parts: modern Cannes to the east and the old Roman hilltop town of Canois Castrum (now known as le Suquet) on a small hill to the west. This district was Cannes' original fishing village and, appropriately, *Le Suquet* is also the Provençal name for a kind of fish soup! Unlike much of the town, it has managed to preserve the air of warmth and intimacy of bygone days. Its lively lanes of fishermen's cottages have been trans-formed into cosy restaurants, and the district is crowned by an imposing castle and watch tower affording sweeping coastal views.

Cannes' castle was constructed by the Lérins monks in the 11th and 12th centuries, together with a small chapel, and houses the **Musée de la Castre** – containing archaeo-logical and ethnographical collections from all over the world. The austere church in the centre of the old town, Notre-Dame d'Espérance, was built in 1648 when the chapel became too small.

At the foot of the hill, in the Vieux Port (Old Port), bobbing fishing craft are juxtaposed with millionaires' yachts. Near by, the daily covered market – Marché Forville – presents mouth-watering displays of regional produce while the allée de la Liberté, shaded by plane trees, provides the backdrop for both *boules* and a vibrant morning flower market.

To the east, modern Cannes is built round la Croisette, Europe's most elegant seaside promenade, lined with palms, grand *belle époque* hotels and the sparkling bay with its golden beaches (of imported sand to cover the natural pebbles!). The main hotels in Cannes have their own beaches, each with bars, restaurants and immaculate rows of coloured parasols and plush mattresses. La Croisette has been a focus for the paparazzi since Brigitte

Did you know ?

The Cannes International Film Festival was founded in 1939 but the outbreak of war led to the postponement of the first festival until 1947. It has taken place here every year during two weeks in May, and attracts famous faces from all around the world. Cinemas all over town screen films from early morning to well into the night, but you are unlikely to get tickets unless you are accompanied by Bardot or Bond 007.

Bardot graced Cannes' beaches in 1953. Today the most likely place to spot celebrities is at the Hôtel Carlton or Hôtel Martinez (➤ 100), especially during the International Film Festival.

This famous film festival is centred around the ugly, ultramodern **Palais des Festivals et des Congrès** on the waterfront near the flower market. Even if you don't meet any movie stars face to face, you can see their handprints immortalised in the paving stones of the allée des Stars – including Polanski, Bronson, Depardieu, even Mickey Mouse.

Above: *there are splendid
views of the Riviera from
this lush peninsula,
crowned by the Villa
Ephrussi de Rothschild*

CAP FERRAT

The most desirable address on the Riviera – the 'Peninsula
of Billionaires' – has long been a favourite haunt of the
world's rich and famous, including Somerset Maugham,
Edith Piaf, the Duke and Duchess of Windsor, Charlie
Chaplin and David Niven.

The cape is smothered in huge villas hidden among
sumptuous, sub-tropical gardens, including the Villa des
Cèdres – one of Europe's most beautiful private botanical
gardens, with 12,000 species of exotic plants – and the
peninsula's finest property, Villa Ephrussi de Rothschild
(► 26). A shaded coastal path from Villefranche around
the cape past countless enticing inlets (ideal for a
refreshing dip) makes a pleasant stroll before lunch in the
former fishing village of St-Jean-Cap-Ferrat.

CORNICHE D'OR (► 17, TOP TEN)

THE CORNICHES

Three famous cliff roads, called la Grande Corniche
(D2564), la Moyenne Corniche (N7) and l'Inférieure
Corniche, traverse the most mountainous and one of the
most scenic stretches of the Riviera from Nice to Menton
via Monaco.

They each zigzag their way along vertiginous ledges at
three different heights. The highest road – la Grande
Corniche – was originally constructed by Napoléon and is
by far the best choice for picnickers and lovers of plants
and wildlife. The lowest route (l'Inférieure) follows the
coastal contours through all the seaside resorts, and is to

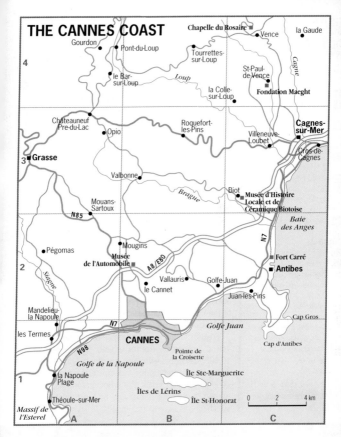

THE CANNES COAST

Chapelle du Rosaire ■ ● Vence   ● la Gaude
Gourdon   ● Pont-du-Loup   Tourrettes-sur-Loup
le Bar-sur-Loup   *Loup*   St-Paul-de-Vence
Châteauneuf Pre-du-Lac   ● Opio   la Colle-sur-Loup   **Fondation Maeght**   *Cagne*
Roquefort-les-Pins   Villeneuve-Loubet   **Cagnes-sur-Mer**
■ 3 **Grasse**   Valbonne   Cros-de-Cagnes
Brague   Biot   **Musée d'Histoire Locale et de Céramique Biotoise**
Mouans-Sartoux   N85   *Baie des Anges*
● Pégomas   Mougins ●   **Musée de l'Automobile** ■   A8/E80   N7   **Fort Carré**   **Antibes**
2   Vallauris ●   Golfe-Juan   Juan-les-Pins
le Cannet   Cap Gros
Mandelieu-la Napoule   N7   *Golfe Juan*   Cap d'Antibes
les Termes   N98   **CANNES**   Pointe de la Croisette
1   la Napoule Plage   *Golfe de la Napoule*   Île Ste-Marguerite
Siagne   *Îles de Lérins*   Île St-Honorat
Théoule–sur-Mer   0   2   4 km
Massif de l'Esterel   **A**   **B**   **C**

be avoided in the main tourist season of July and August. The steep Moyenne at the middle level is undoubtedly the most dramatic. It was on this cliff hanging route, with its hair-raising bends, sudden tunnels and astounding views, that Grace Kelly met her untimely death in 1982. Today the road is frequently used for filming car commercials and movie car chases.

ÈZE (► 18, TOP TEN)

FAYENCE ✪

This large hillside town is a popular centre for local arts. The steep, narrow streets of the old town brim with the ateliers of local artists, weavers, potters, coppersmiths, stone and wood carvers.

Fayence is ringed by a number of picturesque villages, also well known for their arts and crafts – including Tourrettes, Callian, Montauroux and Seillans.

➕ 29C3
ℹ place Léon Roux ☎ 04 94 76 20 08
 Grasse (► 60)
❓ Pays de Fayence music festival in October

➕ 65B3

📍 325 rue Jean-Jaurès

☎ 04 94 17 19 19

🔁 Corniche d'Or (➤ 17)

Arènes de Fréjus

✉ rue Vadon, Provenance
de Puget-sur-Argens

☎ 04 94 17 05 60

🕐 Apr–Sep 9:30–11:45, 2–8;
Oct–Mar 9–11:45,
2–4:15. Closed Tue

♿ None 🎭 Moderate

Cathédrale

✉ place Formigé

🕐 Cathedral: 9–12, 4–6.
Cloisters and baptistry:
Apr–Sep Wed–Mon 9–7;
Oct–Mar 9–12, 2–5.
Closed Tue

♿ Good

🎭 Cathedral: free. Cloisters
and baptistry: expensive

❓ Cloisters and baptistry
guided tours only

*Plane trees shade a
fountain-splashed square
in Fréjus*

FRÉJUS ✪

Now merged together into a holiday conglomeration with
its neighbour St-Raphaël, Fréjus lies at a strategic position
at the mouth of the Argens River between the Massif des
Maures and the Massif de l'Esterel.

It was founded by Julius Caesar in 49 BC as Forum Julii,
an important staging post on the Aurelian Way from Rome
to Arles and the oldest Roman city in Gaul. Under
Augustus it soon became a flourishing naval base, second
in importance only to Marseille, with around 35,000 inhabitants – a population larger than Fréjus' today.

Unfortunately, much of the Roman city was destroyed
by the Saracens in the 10th century, but some vestiges
remain, including sections of the walls and a tower at the
western Porte des Gaules. The opposite entrance to the
east, the Porte de Rome, marks the end of a 40km
aqueduct, with a few ruined arches still visible alongside
the N7. To the north, the semicircular Théâtre Romain still
holds performances in summer, and to the south, remains
of the Praetorium, or military headquarters, of the eastern
citadel can still be seen.

Fréjus' most impressive Roman relic is the deteriorating
1st- to 2nd-century **Arènes** or amphitheatre, built to seat
10,000 spectators. Although substantially damaged, it is
still a popular setting for rock concerts and bullfights. (A
good way to visit some of the Roman remains, which are
spread throughout the city, is by the tourist *petit train*
which runs in summer months.)

The town's pride and joy, however, is the 13th-century **cathedral** in the medieval town. The carved walnut doors at the entrance, dating from the Renaissance, are normally protected behind shutters. They portray scenes of a Saracen massacre and are on view only as part of a guided tour. The tour also visits the medieval cloisters, which surround a tranquil garden of scented shrubbery. Originally the cloisters were two storeys high, but only one of the upper galleries remains, held aloft by slender columns and ornately carved ceilings depicting fantastic animals, monsters and mermaids. The perfectly preserved octagonal baptistry is one of France's oldest.

There is also a small Musée Archéologique within the cathedral illustrating the history of Fréjus with treasures found in the surrounding countryside, including a complete Roman mosaic of a leopard and the famous double-headed bust of Hermes, discovered in 1970 (in fact a copy, as the priceless Hellenistic original is kept securely behind lock and key).

The ancient cathedral dominates the main square in Fréjus

FRÉJUS-PLAGE ✪

Following the decline of the Roman Empire, Fréjus' port lost its significance and became silted up, forming the fine sandy beach of Fréjus-Plage, 2km from the town centre – a modern resort which merges into its eastern neighbour, St-Raphaël. The development of holiday flats, shops, bars and restaurants along the seafront has made Fréjus-Plage a particularly popular resort for families, thanks to its clean albeit crowded beach, its safe swimming and its proximity to the nearby attractions of Aquatic (a water theme park off the RN98) and the Zoo-Safari-Park (next to the A8).

➕ 65B3
ℹ boulevard de la Libération
☎ 04 94 51 48 42
🔄 Corniche d'Or (➤ 17), St-Raphaël (➤ 79)

Fréjus-Plage – always a popular choice for families

Did you know ?

*There are 30 major parfumeries in and around Grasse.
Each employs a head perfumer known as le nez.
There are 300 'noses' in the world, 150 of whom work in
France, 50 in Grasse. Their job is to blend many
different essences to create a new fragrance.
It takes 900,000 rosebuds to produce one litre of essence,
which could cost anything up to F125,000.*

🚩 57A3
ℹ️ 3 place de la Foux
☎ 04 93 36 03 56

**Musée International de la
Parfumerie**
✉ 8 place du Cours
☎ 03 93 36 80 20
🕐 Jun–Sep 10–7; Oct–May
10–12, 2–5. Closed Nov,
Mon, Tue and hols
♿ Very good
💰 Expensive

Maison Fragonard
✉ 20 boulevard Fragonard
☎ 04 93 36 44 65
🕐 Daily
♿ Good
💰 Free

GRASSE

The ancient town of Grasse is a feast for the senses. Visit
on a still day, and you will find sweet floral fragrances
lingering in the air, as Grasse has been the centre of the
world's perfume industry for the past 400 years. Come on
a clear, sunny day, and the memorable views towards the
coast will explain why it has earned the nickname 'Balcony
of the Côte d'Azur'.

The mild climate, rich soil and cradle of mountains
sheltering the town from the harsh north winds, make
Grasse ideal for flower production almost all year round.
Acre upon acre of the surrounding terraced countryside is
used to cultivate aromatic herbs and flowers: mimosa in
spring, roses and jasmine in summer; in the autumn, rows
of purple lavender stripe the landscape above the town.
Until recently around 85 per cent of the world's flower
essence was created here, and even now this sleepy,
fragrance-filled town is France's leading centre for the cut
flower market.

Somewhat surprisingly for such a sweet-scented place,
Grasse started out in the Middle Ages as a tannery town,
filled with all the nauseating smells of the leather industry.
By the 16th century, local Italian glove-makers began to

use local flowers to perfume their gloves (a fashion made popular by Catherine de Medici), and Grasse rapidly became an important perfume centre.

You can learn more about the history of Grasse and the alchemy of the perfume industry at the fascinating **Musée International de la Parfumerie**, which also has an ornate collection of labels, boxes, caskets and scent bottles (including art-nouveau glass by Lalique). The tour ends in the museum's fragrant roof top greenhouse.

There are two main perfume factories in Grasse: the largest, **Maison Fragonard**, is named after a beloved 18th-century local artist, Jean-Honoré Fragonard (whose works can be viewed at the Musée Fragonard), while at Galimard's **Studio des Fragrances**, you can even create your own fragrance.

Apart from the perfumeries, Grasse has an attractive old quarter to explore. The place aux Aires, a lovely fountain-splashed square, is the scene of a vibrant morning flower market. Near by, the austere limestone cathedral of Notre-Dame-de-Puy contains Fragonard's *Lavement des Pieds* (Washing of the Feet) and two treasured Rubens paintings, *Crucifixion* and *Courronnement d'Épines* (Crown of Thorns). At the edge of the old town, the new **Musée Provençal du Costume et du Bijou** and the **Musée d'Art et d'Histoire de Provence** both provide rare insights into local culture, traditions and treasures.

Studio des Fragrances Galimard

- ⊠ route de Pégomas
- ☎ 04 93 09 20 00
- 🕐 Daily by appointment
- ♿ Good
- 💶 Free but it costs F200 to create your own perfume

Musée Provençal du Costume et du Bijou

- ⊠ Hôtel de Clapiers Cabris, 2 rue Jean Ossola
- ☎ 04 93 36 44 65
- 🕐 Daily 10–1, 2–6
- ♿ Good 💶 Free

Musée d'Art et d'Histoire de Provence

- ⊠ 2 rue Mirabeau
- ☎ 04 93 36 01 61
- 🕐 Jun–Sep 10–7; Oct–May 10–12, 2–5. Closed Nov, Mon, Tue and hols
- ♿ Good
- 💶 Moderate

Flowers for sale at the morning market

65B2

1 boulevard des Aliziers
☎ 04 94 43 36 98
↔ Port-Grimaud (➤ 77),
St-Tropez (➤ 80)

GRIMAUD

Grimaud is one of Provence's most photogenic *villages perchés*, crowned by a romantic 11th-century château belonging to the Grimaldi family, after whom the village is named. Hidden amidst flower-filled streets and shaded squares, you will find a beautiful Romanesque church (Église St-Michel), a restored 12th-century mill and, in the arcaded rue des Templiers, a Hospice of the Knights Templars. From the château there are impressive views over Port-Grimaud (➤ 77) and the Gulf of St-Tropez, and inland across the Maures (➤ 64).

ÎLES DE LÉRINS (➤ 21, TOP TEN)

JUAN-LES-PINS

Juan-les-Pins became the first summer resort on the Riviera in the 1920s, thanks to Nice restaurateur Edouard Baudoin, who saw a film about Miami Beach and decided to re-create it on the Côte d'Azur. In 1924, he bought a stretch of land, including a pine grove and a beach of fine silvery sand, and opened a restaurant and a small casino. By 1930 Juan-les-Pins had become not only the most popular resort, but also the most scandal-ridden, as the first beach in France where young women dared to bathe in one-piece swimsuits without skirts.

Today it remains a very popular resort, renowned for its nightlife, with countless cafés, bars and nightclubs all competing with each other on decibel levels. Yet it maintains a certain style and sophistication, thanks to its smart shops, beautiful pine-fringed beach and famous summer jazz festival.

29D2

51 boulevard Guillaumont
☎ 04 92 90 53 05
↔ Antibes (➤ 48), Biot
(➤ 50), Vallauris (➤ 49)
❓ International Jazz Festival
for 2 weeks in July.
Tickets from Maison de
Tourism

Beach addicts enjoy Juan-les-Pins by day, but after sundown is when it really hots up

MANDELIEU-LA NAPOULE ☆

The underrated resorts of Mandelieu-la Napoule lie in the shadow of their glamorous neighbour, Cannes. Inland, Mandelieu is known for golf, boasting one of the largest golf-courses in Europe.

The sister town of la Napoule has three sandy beaches and a large marina, but its main attraction is a seaside fairy-tale castle (**Château-Musée Henri Clews**), built in 1919 by Henry Clews, an American millionaire and sculptor, as a refuge from the modern world. This pseudo-medieval fantasy castle and gardens is decked out with Clews' eccentric sculptures and artwork. Above the entrance is carved his motto 'Once upon a time'.

MASSIF DES MAURES ☆☆

Just inland from the coast, the Maures mountains offer a welcome escape from the tourist hordes of nearby St-Tropez. Its name comes from the Greek *amauros*, meaning dark and sombre, and it is a surprisingly unfrequented region of low hills, clothed in dense forests of cork oaks, conifers and chestnut trees bearing fruits the size of tennis balls. Take time to explore and you will find its deserted, winding roads of seemingly endless woodland are interrupted by the occasional yellow splash of mimosa or a quaint hidden village.

Tranquil **Collobrières** lies alongside the River Collobrier at the heart of the wild Massif. In addition to cork production (► 64) this small village's other major industry is *marrons glacés* and other sweet chestnut confectionery.

Cogolin is one of the main towns of the Maures. Its economy depends on the traditional crafts of cane furniture, silk yarn, brier pipes, knotted wool carpets and, above all, reeds for wind instruments, attracting musicians from afar. The old town is graced with brightly coloured houses ablaze with flowers, narrow cobbled streets and peaceful *placettes* (tiny squares).

🚩 57A1
ℹ️ Mandelieu: avenue de Cannes ☎ 04 93 49 14 39; la Napoule: avenue Henri-Clews ☎ 04 93 49 95 31

Château-Musée Henri Clews
🕐 Mar–Oct, Mon–Fri guided tours at 3PM and 4PM. Closed Tue
♿ Few
💰 Expensive

Collobrières
🚩 65A2
ℹ️ boulevard Charles-Caminat ☎ 04 94 48 08 00

Cogolin
🚩 65B2
ℹ️ place de la République ☎ 04 94 54 63 17

A farmer sells sweet chestnuts freshly picked from the Maures mountains

Massif des Maures

Leave le Lavandou on the D559 heading west. Turn right on to the D41 to Bormes–les–Mimosas (▶ 51) then on to the heart of the Massif up to the Col de Babaou.

The view from here affords spectacular views of the sea, the Îles d'Hyères and the Maures mountains.

The D41 descends towards the Réal Collobrier valley and on (via the D14) to Collobrières.

Distance
115km

Time
Half day

Start/end point
le Lavandou
✚ 28B1

Lunch
La Petite Fontaine,
Collobrières (£)
✉ 1 place de la République
☎ 04 94 48 00 12

Above: *the stripped cork oaks of the Massif are a fascinating sight*

Collobrières is reputed to have been the first place in France to learn about corkage from the Spanish in the Middle Ages, and cork production is still its major industry.

Continue eastwards on the D14 (signed Grimaud). After 6km a narrow road to the right leads to the Chartreuse de la Verne.

This former Carthusian monastery, founded in 1170 in this desolate forest setting, has recently been restored.

Return to the D14, and continue to Grimaud.

Grimaud is one of the most ancient and most picturesque *villages perchés* in the Maures mountains (▶ 62).

Take the D558 southwards to Cogolin.

Although a busy, working town, Cogolin is well worth visiting for its unusual local crafts (▶ 63).

Exit on the N98, up the Môle valley. Turn left into the D27 and wind up the north face of the coastal chain of hills over the Col du Canadel.

The panorama from this pass embraces the Corniche des Maures and the distant Îles d'Hyères.

Turn right on to the forest road to Col de Caguo-Ven. Return to le Lavandou via Bormes–les–Mimosas.

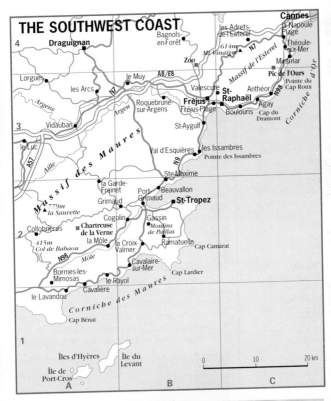

THE SOUTHWEST COAST

Unlike the almost continuous chain of resorts from Menton to Cannes, the southwest region of the Riviera around St-Tropez boasts a wilder, more rugged coastal strip, with deserted creeks and bleached beaches. Its resorts are more strung-out, with stretches of undeveloped countryside in between. St-Tropez (► 80) is the focus for the area.

The interior is also surprisingly undeveloped: the rugged rust-red canyons and dramatic rock formations of the Massif de l'Esterel (► 17) contrast with the thickly forested hills of the Massif des Maures, while the St-Tropez peninsula hides appealing, medieval villages amidst its valued vines.

Bringing in the grape harvest

65

MENTON ❷❷

Only 1.5km from the frontier, it comes as no surprise that Menton is France's most Italianate resort, a picture-postcard jumble of tall, pale ochre houses at the foot of a sheltering mountain backdrop.

Until the mid-19th century, when the Riviera became a fashionable and wealthy winter resort, Menton was a little-known fishing port belonging to the Grimaldis. *Fin de siècle* hotels resembling palaces started to spring up throughout the town. After World War I, Menton lost out to its more glamorous neighbours – Nice, Cannes, St-Tropez and Monaco – although the faded elegance of the *belle époque* is still apparent.

By contrast, the medieval old town is a hotchpotch of ancient pastel-coloured houses dissected by terracotta-paved steps, alleys and tiny squares. There are two magnificent baroque churches: St-Michel and the Chapelle de la Conception, with finely ornamented façades. Between them, the Parvis St-Michel, a mosaic square of black and white cobbles depicting the Grimaldi coat of arms, provides a delightful setting for the summer Chamber Music Festival.

On the site of the ancient castle at the top of the old town, a fascinating cemetery with sweeping sea views reflects the cosmopolitanism of the town at the end of the last century, and was described by writer Guy de Maupassant as 'the most aristocratic in Europe' (➤ 68). Other notable sights include the **Musée de la Préhistoire**

➕ 72C2

ℹ️ Palais de l'Europe, avenue Boyer ☎ 04 92 41 76 76

🚌 Peille, Peillon, Ste-Agnes (Drive ➤ 73), Roquebrune-Cap-Martin (➤ 78)

❓ Ten-day Lemon Festival (Fête du Citron) in Feb; Music Festival in Aug

Musée de la Préhistoire Régional

✉️ rue Lorédan Larchey

☎ 04 93 35 84 64

🕐 16 Sep–14 Jun 10–12, 2–6; 15 Jun–15 Sep 10–12, 3–7. Closed Tue and hols

♿ Few

💶 Free

Palais Carnolès
Musée des Beaux-Arts

✉️ 3 avenue de la Madone

☎ 04 93 35 49 71

🕐 16 Sep–14 Jun 10–12, 2–6; 15 Jun–15 Sep 10–12, 3–7. Closed Tue and hols

♿ Good

💶 Free

❓ Free access also to the citrus gardens

Musée Jean Cocteau

✉️ quai Napoléon III

☎ 04 93 57 72 30

🕐 16 Sep–14 Jun 10–12, 2–6; 15 Jun–15 Sep 10–12, 3–7. Closed Tue and hols

♿ Few

💶 Free (small donations requested)

Menton – one of the Riviera's most popular moorings

Régional, **Palais Carnolès**, the sumptuous 18th-century summer residence of the Princes of Monaco, now Menton's main art museum; and the **Musée Jean Cocteau**, dedicated to the town's most famous son. Cocteau also decorated the remarkable **Salle des Mariages** in the Hôtel de Ville, reflecting romantic, spiritual and ironic images of matrimony.

Menton is France's warmest town, boasting an annual 300 days of sun and as a result the town is bursting with semi-tropical gardens. Most of them are in the wealthy Garavan district in the foothills behind the town near the Italian border, notably the charming Jardin Botanique, the ancient olive grove of Parc du Pian and the Valencian Jardin Fontana Rosa, dedicated to writers by Spanish author Blasso Ibánez.

Menton is also the 'lemon capital of the world', and the terraced slopes behind are covered in citrus groves. The garden surrounding the Palais Carnolès claims to be the largest citrus fruit garden in Europe. The Biovès garden in the town centre, fancifully bordered with palms and lemon trees, is the venue in February of Menton's spectacular Fête du Citron (Lemon Festival), with its amazing garden displays and procession of floats made out of 130 tonnes of golden citrus fruits.

Salle des Mariages

✉ Hôtel de Ville, place Ardoïno
☎ 04 92 10 50 00
🕐 8:30–12:30, 1:30–5. Closed Sat, Sun and hols
♿ Very good
💶 Cheap

An elaborate display at Menton's Lemon Festival

Vieux Menton & the Gardens of Garavan

Start on the promenade du Soleil outside the Musée Jean Cocteau. Follow the coast eastwards along quai Benett and promenade de la Mer past the Vieux Port (Old Port).

Mornings are always busiest at the Vieux Port, with fishermen repairing their nets and a small daily fish market.

Continue until Marché-U supermarket. Cross the main road (porte de France) and head up avenue St-Jacques.

On the left is the Jardin Botanique (➤ 67), and to the right the Parc du Pian (➤ 67).

Go up some steps, then turn left along boulevard de Garavan. Continue some distance until you reach place du Cimetière at the top.

Distance
4km

Time
2 hours

Start/end point
Musée Jean Cocteau, quai Napoléon III
⊞ 72C2

Lunch
Choice of restaurants and cafés (£–££) in place du Cap

Look out here for the graves of such celebrities as William Webb Ellis, inventor of rugby, illustrator Aubrey Beardsley and Rasputin's assassin, Prince Youssoupov.

From place du Cimetière, go down the pedestrian rue du Vieux-Château, leaving the cemetery to your right. Zigzag down the stepped alley into place de la Conception.

Here are Vieux Menton's two main churches (➤ 66).

Cross the square and descend the 104 steps of steep, narrow rue des Écoles Pies. Turn right at the huilerie. Head halfway down the road (towards Chapelle des Pénitents Noirs at the end) then first left down traverse rue de Bréa to rue St-Michel.

Rue St-Michel is Menton's lively pedestrian thoroughfare.

Above: fishermen still use traditional methods to repair their nets

Turn left then cross place du Cap, leaving restaurant L'Olivier to your left. Turn immediately right under an arch along rue du Bastion back to the promenade du Soleil.

Monaco

The Principality of Monaco is the world's second smallest sovereign state after the Vatican – a 195ha, spotlessly clean strip of skyscraper-clad land squeezed between sea and mountains on largely reclaimed land. It is a magnet for the world's jet-setters, attracted by the lack of taxes and the world's highest incomes.

Only 6,000 of Monaco's 30,000 residents are Monégasque. The remainder are all prepared to pay exorbitant prices for a cramped high-rise apartment in order to be part of Monaco's famed community of millionaires, gamblers, 'offshore' bankers and princesses.

With so much evident wealth and glamour, it is hard to imagine Monaco's turbulent past. At various times occupied by the French, the Spanish and the Dukes of Savoy, for the last 700 years the principality has been ruled by the Grimaldi family, the world's oldest reigning monarchy, in power ever since 1297 when a Grimaldi known as Francesco 'the Spiteful' dressed up as a friar and knocked at the door of Monaco's Ghibelline fortress asking for hospitality, together with his men, disguised as monks. Once inside, they killed the guards and took control of the garrison. Hence the two sword-brandishing monks on the Grimaldi family crest.

🔢 72C2

ℹ️ 2a boulevard des Moulins

☎ 377/92 16 61 16

🔄 Cap Ferrat (▶ 56), the Corniches (▶ 56), Éze (▶ 18), Menton (▶ 66), Nice (▶ 30), Villefranche (▶ 90)

Below: *the view from Monaco-Ville down to the harbour and Monte-Carlo*

Inset: *The Grimaldi crest*

This statue of Princess Grace adorns her memorial rose garden

The Grimaldis once ruled an area which extended along the coast from Antibes to Menton. However, their high taxes provoked a revolt, and the principality shrank to its present size. In the mid-19th century, Prince Charles III of Monaco, facing a financial crisis, opened the Casino to increase revenue. It was such a success that taxes were soon abolished altogether. Charles was succeeded by Prince Albert I, who introduced numerous academic and scientific institutions, including the Musée Océanographique. Since 1949, Monaco has been ruled by Prince Rainier Louis Henri Maxence Bertrand de Grimaldi, the 26th ruling prince of the Grimaldi family, who has invested considerably in the modernisation of the principality.

In 1956, Prince Rainier added fairy-tale cachet to his realm by marrying the legendary American film star Grace Kelly, who met with a tragic car accident in 1982 along la Moyenne Corniche. Their son Albert is heir to the throne, making him the Riviera's most sought-after bachelor, although Stéphanie and Caroline, his sometimes wayward sisters, tend to dominate the press.

Even though Monaco is so small, finding your way around can prove difficult. Not only is Monaco the name of the principality, but Monaco-Ville is also a district on the peninsula to the south, containing the old town with its narrow streets. By startling contrast, the newer high-rise district of Monte-Carlo to the east is centred round the Casino and designer shops. The port quarter, between Monte-Carlo and Monaco-Ville, is called la Condamine, and there is a largely industrial district, Fontvieille, to the southwest.

Left: *the unusual cathedral – an oasis of calm in Monaco-Ville*

Far left: *changing the guard at the Palace*

What to See in Monaco

CASINO (▶ 16, TOP TEN)

CATHÉDRALE ✪✪
Built in 1875 (and funded by Casino profits!), this ostentatious neo-Romanesque cathedral has among its treasures two 16th-century retables by Niçoise artist Louis Bréa, and the tomb of the still much-mourned Princess Grace.

✉ 4 rue Colonel Bellando de Castro, Monaco-Ville
🚌 1, 2
♿ Good
🎟 Free

LA CONDAMINE ✪✪
In medieval times, la Condamine referred to cultivable land at the foot of a village or a castle. Today this area, at the foot of the royal palace, is a busy commercial district wrapped around the port of Monaco. It is fun to wander along the quayside, to marvel at the size and cost of the yachts, but take time to explore the back streets too, for they hide some superb shops and restaurants.

🚌 1,2,5,6
🚢 Apr–Sep: daily excursions round the Rock, or further afield to Îles de Lérins, St-Tropez or San Remo in Italy ✉ quai des Etats-Unis Port d'Hercule
☎ 377/92 16 15 15

FONTVIEILLE ✪✪
This zone of modern residential and commercial development, built on reclaimed land below the rock of Monaco-Ville, has a marina, sports stadium, and excellent shops; it also has a fine park, and the Princess Grace Rose Garden, a peaceful oasis fragrant with the scent of 4,000 rose trees.

The terraces of Fontvieille were purpose-built to house numerous museums, including Prince Rainier's private collection of classic cars, a **Naval Museum**, with 180 models of famous ships, a stamp and coin museum, and even a zoo.

Collection de Voitures
☎ 377/92 05 28 56
🕐 10–6. Closed Nov
🚌 5, 6
♿ Good
🎟 Very expensive

Musée Naval
☎ 377/92 05 28 48
🕐 10–6
🚌 5, 6
♿ Good
🎟 Expensive

JARDIN EXOTIQUE DE MONEGHETTI ✪✪
Just off the Moyenne Corniche, above Fontvieille, lies one of Monaco's finest attractions, the **Exotic Garden**, containing several thousand cacti and succulents of vivid colours and amazing shapes (some nearly 10m high).

🕐 15 May–15 Sep 9–7 (6 nightfall in winter)
🚌 2 ♿ Few
🎟 Very expensive

71

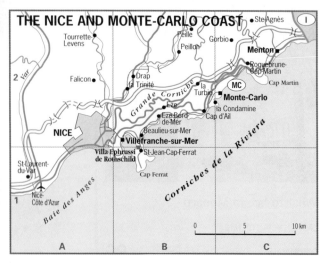

THE NICE AND MONTE-CARLO COAST

Ste-Agnès

Tourrette-Levens
Péille
Peillon
Gorbio
Menton
Roquebrune-Cap-Martin
Cap Martin

2 Var
Falicon
Drap
la Trinité
Grande Corniche
la Turbie
MC
Monte-Carlo
Èze
Èze-Bord-de-Mer
la Condamine
Cap d'Ail
Beaulieu-sur-Mer
Villefranche-sur-Mer

NICE

Villa Ephrussi de Rothschild
St-Jean-Cap-Ferrat
Corniches de la Riviera

St-Laurent-du-Var
Cap Ferrat
Nice-Côte d'Azur
Baie des Anges

0   5   10 km

A   B   C

Monte-Carlo Story

📧 terrasses du parking du Chemin des Pêcheurs
☎ 377/93 25 32 33
🕐 Mar–Oct 11–5
🍴 1,2 ♿ Very good
💰 Very expensive

Musée du Vieux Monaco

📧 rue Emile de Loth
☎ 377/93 50 57 28
🕐 Open by appointment
🍴 1, 2
♿ Few 💰 Free

📧 place du Palais
☎ 377/93 25 18 31
🕐 Jun–Sep 9:30–6:30; Oct 10–5. Closed Nov–May
🍴 1,2 ♿ Few
💰 Expensive

Guarding the Grimaldi home, the Palais du Prince

MONACO-VILLE ✪✪

The labyrinth of cool, cobbled streets perched on 'the Rock' (a sheer-sided finger of land extending 800m into the sea) has been well preserved, with lovely fountain-filled squares and fine Italianate façades – although, inevitably, the shops around the royal palace purvey the usual tacky souvenirs. Look out for the **Multi-vision Monte-Carlo Story** and the fascinating **Musée du Vieux Monaco**, portraying life on the Rock throughout the centuries. The Historial des Princes de Monaco depicts historical episodes in the Grimaldi dynasty through life-sized wax models.

MUSÉE OCÉANOGRAPHIQUE (➤ 24, TOP TEN)

PALAIS DU PRINCE ✪✪

Guided tours take visitors through the priceless treasures of the state apartments and the small Musée Napoléon in the south wing of the palace, when Prince Rainier is away in summer. When he is in residence, the royal colours are flown from the tower, and visitors must be content with the changing of the guard ceremony which is held every morning at 11:55.

Circular Drive from Monaco

The D53 zigzags for 6km high above Monaco to la Turbie.

La Turbie is easily recognisable due to the huge Roman monument, the Trophée des Alpes, built in honour of Emperor Augustus, who captured this Alpine region in the 1st century BC.

Exit la Turbie on the D53 (direction Peille). The road winds inland through wild countryside to Peille.

Peille (► 76) is full of surprises: ancient mansions redolent of a noble past; attractive squares adorned with Gothic fountains, arches and urns; even an old salt-tax office.

Backtrack south, along the D53 again. Turn left along the D22 through barren garrigue scrub, over the Col de La Madone and through a small forest to Ste–Agnès.

At 650m, Ste-Agnès is the highest village on the Riviera, and rated 'one of the most beautiful villages in France'.

Take the D22 towards Menton. Immediately after crossing the autoroute, take a tiny unsignposted lane on the right (the Chemin des Vignes) to Gorbio.

The best time to visit medieval Gorbio is in June, when the Snail Festival takes place and the streets are lit with thousands of tiny lamps made from snail shells.

Leave Gorbio along avenue Aristide Briand (signed Grande Corniche). Turn left on to the D2564 to Roquebrune old village (► 78).

Don't miss the splendid view from Roquebrune castle's terrace over sloping orange roofs past dark cypress trees to the sparkling sea beyond.

Return on the D2564 towards la Turbie. Turn left after Hôtel Le Vista Palace (D51) and on to Monaco via the RN7.

Rising 480m above sea level, the lofty Trophée des Alpes put la Turbie on the map

Distance
66km

Time
2 hours; full day with visits

Start/end point
Monaco
✚ 72C2

Lunch
La Vieille Auberge (£)
✉ Ste-Agnès
☎ 04 93 35 92 02

In the Know

If you have only a short time to visit the French Riviera, or would like to get a real flavour of the country, here are some ideas:

10
Ways to Be a Local

Shop in local markets and sample the food before you buy.

Try your hand at *boules* in a shady village square.

While away the hours in the local village bar.

Develop a taste for local wines and pastis.

Chat to locals about culinary delights, sport and politics.

Remember to address people as *monsieur, madame* or *mademoiselle.*

How to look cool in St-Tropez

Sunbathe topless (but don't walk around town in beachwear afterwards)!

Relish the local cuisine and enjoy leisurely meals.

Relax, be idle, unwind and settle into the Provençal pace of life.

Take a siesta.

10
Top Beaches

Cap d'Antibes, Plage de la Garoupe – best alternative to your own private stretch of beach on the Cap.

Cannes – best for star-spotting.

Esterel Massif – plenty of sandy coves with a backdrop of red porphyry rock, particularly east of Le Trayas.

Fréjus-Plage – best for families.

Îles de Lérins – best island beaches.

Juan-les-Pins – best sandy beach.

Menton – best sunshine record.

Nice (Ruhl-Plage) – best watersports and the first beach on the coast to be on the Internet. Surf under the shade of beach umbrellas!

St-Tropez (La Voile Rouge) – the trendiest and the most frivolous.

St-Tropez (Plage de la Briande) – the most deserted.

10
Top View Points

The summit of Mont Vinaigre in the Massif de l'Esterel (► 17).

The Exotic Gardens in Èze – (► 18) across to Corsica.

Frequent viewpoints along the Grande Corniche (► 56).

The highest point of the village of Gourdon (► 88).

The D53 road looking down over Monaco.

The Colline du Château in Nice (► 36).

The church tower in Port-Grimaud (► 77).

The outdoor lift at La Vista Palace hotel, Roquebrune, behind Monte-Carlo. Go in for a drink!

The Chemin des Collines, La Californie, in Super-Cannes, where the wealthiest of Cannes' residents live.

Les Moulins de Paillas on the St-Tropez peninsula (► 85).

10
Top Parks and Gardens

Beaulieu-sur-Mer – Villa Kérylos (► 50).

Biot – Bonsaï Arboretum of the Côte d'Azur ✉ 299 chemin du Val de Pôme.

Cagnes-sur-Mer – Renoir's Garden (► 52).

Èze – Jardin Exotique (► 18).

Mandelieu-la Napoule – Gardens of the Château-Musée Henri Clews (► 63).

Monaco's Jardin Exotique – a mecca for all gardeners

Menton – Citrus Garden, Palais Carnolès (► 67).

Monaco – Jardin Exotique (► 71).

Nice – Phoenix Parc Floral.

St-Jean-Cap-Ferrat – Villa Ephrussi de Rothschild (► 26).

St-Paul-de-Vence – gardens of Fondation Maeght (► 20).

5
Top Activities

Go fishing and cook your catch on board (Sea Cruises Golfe-Juan ☎ 93 42 08 45).

Take a boat trip to Corsica from Nice's old port (SNCM ☎ 04 93 13 66 66).

Visit the Îles de Lérins (Compagnie Maritime Cannoise ☎ 04 93 38 66 33).

Hire a Harley-Davidson and cruise the streets of St-Tropez (St-Tropez Cars ☎ 04 94 97 10 34).

Take a helicopter from Nice airport to Monte-Carlo (Héli Inter Riviera ☎ 04 93 21 46 46).

5
Top Ice-cream Parlours

Antibes – Galateria Italiana ✉ place Nationale.

Juan-les-Pins – Café de la Plage ✉ 1 boulevard Edouard Baudoin.

Nice – Fenocchio ✉ place Rossetti (► 93).

St-Raphael – Baudeno ✉ Vieux Port.

St-Tropez – Sénéquier ✉ quai Suffren (► 98).

Join the locals and take the time to watch the world go by

29D2

avenue Charles Mallet

☎ 04 93 75 87 67

Musée de la Photographie

✉ porte Sarrazine, Mougins

☎ 04 93 75 85 67

🕐 Daily 1–7; Jul–Aug 2–11. Closed Tue

♿ Few

💲 Moderate

MOUGINS

Outwardly Mougins seems a typical Provençal hill village but, once inside its medieval ramparts, you will find one of the Riviera's smartest villages, whose past residents have included Jacques Brel, Yves Saint Laurent, Catherine Deneuve and Picasso – who spent the last 12 years of his life here. Numerous celluloid portraits of him can be seen in the **Musée de la Photographie**.

Mougin's main attraction, though, is the sheer number of renowned restaurants. People come from miles around to dine at Le Relais, La Ferme de Mougins, Le Mas Candille or, for a real treat, Le Moulin de Mougins (➤ 97), which is considered to be one of the world's most prestigious gourmet temples.

72B2

Mairie ☎ 04 93 91 90 01

❓ Ask for the key of the church of Ste-Marie at the hospice

Sun and shade define the cobbled streets of Peille

PEILLE

Just a short distance inland and set in wild, underpopulated countryside, Peille is a perfect retreat from the touristic frenzy of the coast, a unique *village perché*, with its own Provençal dialect, Pelhasc.

Peille had unusual ideas on religion too. During the Middle Ages, it was excommunicated several times rather than pay the bishop's tithes. The Chapelle des Pénitents Noirs was converted into a communal oil press and its splendid domed Chapelle de St-Sébastien into the Hôtel de Ville.

Inside the church of Ste-Marie is an interesting painting of the village in medieval times, showing the now-ruined castle in its former glory. Once, during a drought, Peille asked a local shepherd for help. He made it rain on condition that the lord of the castle agreed to give him his daughter's hand in marriage – an event still celebrated on the first Sunday in September.

PEILLON

Peille's twin and neighbouring village, Peillon is one of the Riviera's most beautiful *villages perchés*, very cleverly camouflaged against the landscape. Medieval perched villages were built in lofty positions for safety. From behind their thick ramparts, villagers could keep vigil over the hinterland as well as the coast.

Pellion's huddle of cobbled alleys, steps and arches lead up to a charming little church at the summit. But the main attraction here is the Chapelle des Pénitents Blancs just outside the village, with 15th-century frescoes by Giovanni Canavesio depicting the Passion of Christ. Beyond the chapel, a footpath walk to Peille takes about two hours along what was once a Roman road.

72B2

Mairie ☎ 04 93 79 91 04

? Telephone in advance to arrange a visit to the Chapelle des Pénitents Blancs

PORT-GRIMAUD ✪✪✪

Port-Grimaud is the ultimate property development on the Riviera – a modern mini-Venice of pastel-coloured designer villas on a series of islets, divided by canals and linked by shaded squares and neat bridges. This 'film-set' village, the brainchild of François Spoerry, was built in 1968, and has since become one of France's major tourist attractions. Prices for the 2,500 canalside houses (all with private moorings) are absurdly high, but after all they're just up the road from St-Tropez. Many residents, including Joan Collins, simply jet in for their summer holidays.

The whole port is traffic-free and best explored by water-taxi (*coche d'eau*). At the centre of the village, on its own islet, the pseudo-Romanesque church of St-François-d'Assise contains stained glass by Hungarian-born Victor Vasarély and provides a sweeping view of the port from the top of its tower.

65B2

1 boulevard des Aliziers, Grimaud ☎ 04 94 43 36 98

Grimaud (➤ 62), Massif des Maures (➤ 63), Ste-Maxime (➤ 79), St-Tropez (➤ 80)

? Tourist train links Port-Grimaud to Grimaud

Palatial quayside residences line the canals of Port-Grimaud

Take time to explore old Roquebrune's narrow lanes

✚ 72C2

ℹ promenade Simon-Lorière ☎ 04 94 96 19 24

❓ Markets: food and flowers daily; crafts on Thu; bric-a-brac on Fri

ROQUEBRUNE-CAP-MARTIN ✪✪

Located on a prime site between Menton and Monaco, Roquebrune-Cap-Martin is divided into two areas: old Roquebrune, an attractive medieval *village perché*, and the smart coastal resort of Cap Martin.

Old Roquebrune is a fascinating tangle of ancient flower-filled lanes, stairways and vaulted passages clustered around its castle, the oldest feudal château remaining in France and the sole example of Carolingian style. Built in the 10th century to ward off Saracen attack, it was later remodelled by the Grimaldis, and restored in 1911 by Lord Ingram, one of the first wave of wealthy tourist residents drawn to stylish Cap Martin.

Other visitors attracted to Cap Martin included Queen Victoria, Sir Winston Churchill, Coco Chanel and architect Le Corbusier, who drowned off the cape in 1965 and lies buried in Roquebrune cemetery. A delightful coastal path in his honour (promenade Le Corbusier) circles the cape, past sumptuous villas shrouded in dense foliage.

✚ 57C4

ℹ Maison de la tour, 2 rue Grande ☎ 04 93 32 86 95

↔ Biot (➤ 50); Cagnes (➤ 52); Vence (➤ 89); Villeneuve-Loubet (➤ 90)

ST-PAUL-DE-VENCE ✪✪✪

This large picture-postcard *village perché*, draped gently over a hill close to Cagnes, was appointed a 'Royal Town' by King François in the 16th century, and the wealth of the village is still apparent.

In the 1920s St-Paul was discovered by a group of young, impoverished artists – Signac, Bonnard, Modigliani and Soutine – who stayed at the modest Auberge de la Colombe d'Or, paying for their lodgings with their paintings. Word of the *auberge* spread and soon other artists and young intellectuals arrived. Today the exclusive Hôtel La Colombe d'Or boasts an impressive past guest

list including Braque, Camus, Derain, Maeterlinck, Matisse, Kipling, Picasso and Utrillo and, as a result, one of the finest private collections of modern art in France.

The village perché of St-Paul-de-Vence stands proud on the hillside

The village is still an artists' colony, although perhaps better described as a tourist honeypot, with coach-loads flocking to the Fondation Maeght (▶ 20) and to the smart shops and galleries which line its steep, cobbled streets. However, in spite of the crowds, it remains one of Provence's most exquisite villages, especially at night when the narrow alleys are lit with tiny lanterns.

Did you know ?

A word of warning! In 1993 the Mayor of St-Raphaël reinstated an ancient decree forbidding people to walk around town in swimsuits, so make sure you cover up when not on the beach. The same is true of Ste-Maxime, where there is a fine of F75 for scantily clad tourists.

STE-MAXIME

Ste-Maxime, with its palm-lined promenade, its golden sandy beach, top watersports facilities, vibrant nightlife and popular casino, is the Riviera's archetypal family resort. Admittedly, it lacks the glamour and celebrity status of neighbouring St-Tropez, but it does provide a frequent boat service for star-struck holiday-makers wishing to commute across the bay and, in exchange, it welcomes St-Tropez' overflow of fashionable visitors to its glut of hotels, restaurants and cafés.

🚩 65B2
🛈 promenade Simon-Lorière ☎ 04 94 96 19 24

ST-RAPHAËL

Napoléon put St-Raphaël on the map when he landed here on his return from Egypt in 1799. It developed into a fashionable seaside resort in the 19th century. Unfortunately many of the grand *belle époque* hotels were destroyed during World War II but it still remains popular with families, mainly because of its large sandy beach.

🚩 65C3
🛈 place de la Gare ☎ 04 94 19 52 52

St-Tropez

This charming fishing port, which reached the height of international fame in the 'swinging' sixties, continues to attract the rich and famous, even though its hedonistic image has become a little stale, this tourist honeypot remains one of the most seductive resorts of the entire Riviera.

The old fishing port of St-Tropez remains unchanged despite the razzmatazz

It is fun to rub shoulders with the glitterati in the waterfront cafés, and to wonder at the grandiose yachts moored before the distinctive backdrop of pink and yellow pastel-hued houses, reconstructed after being destroyed in 1944. But take time to explore the maze of narrow streets and squares of old St-Tropez, where there is a village-like atmosphere with markets, chic boutiques and bistros.

The town has long been a popular meeting place for artists. Liszt and de Maupassant were its first celebrities in the 1880s, followed by the painter Signac a decade later. Soon the works of Matisse, Bonnard, Utrillo and Dufy were to immortalise the town on canvas. Painters were followed by an influx of writers between the wars – Colette, Cocteau and Anaïs Nin. Then in the 1950s it was the turn of the film stars, led by the famous Tropezienne, Brigitte Bardot, whose film *Et Dieu Créa La Femme* (1956) marked the start of a new, permissive era.

St-Tropez' star-studded list of residents includes Elton John, Jean-Paul Belmondo and Jean Michel Jarre and, everything here continues to be extravagant, decadent and excessive. Little wonder the French endearingly call it St 'Trop' ('too much').

A Walk Around St-Tropez

Start on the waterfront. Beside the tourist office, go through the porte de la Poissonnerie, past the marble slabs of the daily fish market into place aux Herbes.

The colourful daily fish, fruit and vegetable stalls, just a stone's throw from the glitz and glamour of the quayside, remind visitors of St-Tropez' humble origins as a fishing village.

Leave the square up the steps of rue du Marché, turn left into rue des Commerçants, first right into rue du Clocher to the Église de St-Tropez (▶ 83). Continue along rue Cdt Guichard to place de la Mairie and place Garrezio.

Preparing for the day's catch

These two squares are dominated by the handsome pink and green town hall, and the Tour de Suffren (▶ 84), once home of the great 18th-century Admiral Suffren.

Return past the town hall and along rue de la Ponche. The 15th-century Porche de la Ponche archway leads to the old Ponche quarter.

This is the old fishing district of St-Tropez, centred on the sun-baked place du Révelin, overlooking the unspoilt fishing port and tiny pebble beach.

Head up rue des Ramparts, turn right at rue d'Aumale to the delightful place de l'Ormeau, and left up rue de l'Ormeau to rue de la Citadelle. Turn downhill towards the port, then take the first left into rue Portail du Neuf and turn right at rue Miséricorde.

The Chapelle de la Miséricorde with its quaint bell-tower dates from the 17th century and the road alongside passes through its flying buttresses. The chapel's entrance is on rue Gambetta.

Continue along rue Gambetta for lunch at place des Lices.

Distance
1½km

Time
1½–2 hours, depending on church visits

Start point
waterfront

End point
place des Lices
(▶ 83)

Coffee/lunch
Café des Arts (£)
✉ place des Lices
☎ 04 94 97 02 25

What to See in St-Tropez

Les Graniers
✉ plage des Graniers
☎ 04 94 97 38 50

Club 55
✉ boulevard Patch
☎ 04 94 79 80 14

Tahiti Plage
✉ route de Tahiti
☎ 04 94 97 18 02

Voile Rouge
✉ route des Tamaris
☎ 04 94 97 84 34

✉ montée de la Citadelle
☎ 04 94 97 59 43
🕐 Mid-Jun to mid-Sep 10–6;
winter 10–5. Closed Tue
♿ Few 💲 Very expensive

*Early morning at one
of St-Tropez' chic
beach resorts*

BEACHES ✪✪✪

St-Tropez owes much of its attraction to its gorgeous sandy beaches, for it was here that girls first dared to bathe topless in the 1960s. In total, there are over 6km of enticing golden sand situated on the Baie de Pampelonne, neatly divided into invididual beaches, each with a different character. In summer there's a frequent minibus to the bay from place des Lices.

Les Graniers is the most crowded beach and within easy walking distance of the village; trendy **Club 55** caters for the Paris set; **Tahiti Plage** was once the movie stars' favourite (the original beach bar was constructed from an old film set!), but nowadays star-spotters have more luck at the frivolous **Voile Rouge**. For privacy and seclusion, Plage de la Briande is considered by many to be the best beach in the region, situated halfway along the 19km coastal path that rounds the St-Tropez peninsula.

LA CITADELLE ✪✪

It is worth visiting this 16th-century hilltop fortress for the view alone, which embraces the orange curved-tile roofs of St-Tropez' old town, the dark and distant Maures and Esterel hills, and the shimmering blue of the bay, flecked with sails. The maritime museum in the citadel keep is an annexe of the Musée de la Marine in the Palais de Chaillot in Paris. The museum displays models of ships (including a reconstruction of a Grecian galley), engravings and seascapes of St-Tropez, illustrating the town's long and glorious history, up to the 1944 Allied landings that unfortunately destroyed much of the town.

> ### Did you know ?
>
> *Guy de Maupassant described St-Tropez in the 1880s as 'An enchanting and simple daughter of the sea, one of the modest little towns that have grown in the water like a shellfish, fed on fish and sea air, which produces sailors. It smells of fish and burning tar, brine and boats. Sardine scales glisten like pearls on the cobblestones.'*

ÉGLISE DE ST-TROPEZ

St-Tropez owes its name to a Roman centurion called Torpes, martyred under Nero in AD 68. His head was buried in Pisa then his body was put in a boat with a dog and cockerel who should have devoured it. Surprisingly, when the boat was washed up here, his body remained miraculously untouched.

For over 400 years, the town's most important festival – the Bravade de Saint Torpes, which takes part from 16 to 18 May – has been celebrated in his honour. A gilt bust of Saint Torpes and a model of his boat can be seen in the 19th-century baroque-style church, with its distinctive pink and yellow bell-tower.

🖂 rue de l'Église
🕐 Daily
↔ Tour Suffren (➤ 84),
Vieux Port (➤ 84)

Below: *card players while away the day in the place des Lices*

MUSÉE DE L'ANNONCIADE

Here in this former 16th-century chapel is one of the finest collections of French late 19th- and early 20th-century paintings and bronzes. At that time, St-Tropez was an extremely active centre for the artistic avant-garde and, as a result, most of the hundred or so canvases here belong to the great turn-of-the-century movements of pointillism and fauvism.

Many of the paintings portray local scenes. Be sure to seek out Paul Signac's *L'Orage* (1895), Bonnard's *Le Port de St-Tropez* (1899), Camoin's *La Place des Lices* (1925), works by Dufy, Derain and Vuillard – and the museum cat, called Matisse!

🖂 place Georges Grammont
☎ 04 94 97 04 01
🕐 Jun–Sep 10–12, 3–7;
Oct–May 10–12, 2–6.
Closed Tue, 1 Jan, 1
May, Ascension, Nov, 25
Dec
♿ Few
💷 Expensive
↔ Vieux Port (➤ 84)

PLACE DES LICES

Here is the real heart of St-Tropez, which is still very much as it looked in Camoin's *La Place des Lices* of 1925 (see above), lined with ancient plane trees and Bohemian cafés. Visit on Tuesday or Saturday for its colourful market, or any day to enjoy a game of *boules* and partake of a glass of pastis with the locals.

🍴 Cafés and restaurants
(£-£££)
♿ Good
❓ Shuttle buses run to the beaches in summer

TOUR DE SUFFREN ✪

This massive defensive tower is all that remains of St-Tropez' oldest building, Château de Suffren, constructed in AD 990 by Count Guillaume I of Provence. It is named after the great 18th-century seaman, Admiral Suffren, a native of St-Tropez and one of the most influential admirals of the French fleet. A statue has been erected in his honour on the quay.

VIEUX PORT (OLD PORT) ✪✪✪

It is easy to see why the appealing, pastel-painted houses and crowded cafés that line the quayside have enticed visitors and inspired artists and writers for over a century.

The waterfront today is very much the place to see and be seen in St-Tropez. Try to arrive in an Aston Martin, on a Harley-Davidson, or better still in an enormous gin palace, and remember to moor stern-to, to give onlookers a perfect view! It's always great fun to wander along the quayside, marvelling at luxury yachts the size of ships, and goggling at their decadent millionaire owners tucking into langoustines on deck, served, of course, by the white-frocked crew.

For an overview of the port and all St-Tropez, the harbour breakwater (Môle Jean-Réveille) provides excellent photo opportunities.

ST-TROPEZ PENINSULA ✪✪

Just a short distance inland from St-Tropez – the Riviera's capital of 'see-and-be-seen' – lies a surprisingly undeveloped, uncrowded peninsula splashed with wild flowers and striped with vineyards.

In their midst, the ancient hilltop village of **Gassin**, once a Moorish stronghold, was built as a look-out point during the time of the Saracen invasions. Today it is a colourful Provençal village, blessed with more than its fair share of smart boutiques and restaurants thanks to its proximity to St-Tropez.

Neighbouring **Ramatuelle** was named 'God's Gift' (Rahmatu'llah) by the Saracens and, together with Gassin, is one of the most fashionable

places in the region to own a *résidence secondaire*. Every summer the village hosts popular jazz and theatre festivals.

The countryside surrounding Ramatuelle is swathed in vines, which produce some of Provence's most coveted wines. On the road (D89) between Gassin and Ramatuelle, three ancient windmills, les Moulins de Paillas, offer memorable views of the coast and the surrounding countryside, notably the twin peaks la Sauvette (779m) and Notre-Dame-des-Anges (780m), the highest points in the Massif des Maures.

To the south, **la Croix-Valmer** is surrounded by wild, rocky woodlands. It is said that when Emperor Constantine passed through with his troops on his way to battle in Rome to claim the Empire, he had a vision of a cross over the sea, with the words 'In hoc signo vinces' ('in this sign you will conquer'), prophesying his conversion to Christianity, followed ultimately by all of Europe. A stone cross here commemorates the legend that gave the village its name.

la Croix-Valmer
- 65B2
- rue Martin
- 04 94 79 66 44
- Massif des Maures (► 63)

Photogenic Ramatuelle – a typical Provençal hilltop village

Food & Drink

France is universally recognised as the world leader in the field of food and wine, and of all its great regional styles *la cuisine Provençale* has one of the strongest personalities – piquant, aromatic Mediterranean dishes with bold, sun-drenched colours and strong earthy flavours as varied as its landscapes.

Garlic and olives – the taste of Provence

Provençal Specialities

Most Provençal dishes rely heavily on garlic, tomatoes, olive oil, onions and wild herbs (thyme, rosemary, sage and basil). Specialities include *soupe au pistou* (vegetable soup with cheese, garlic and basil; *beignets de courgettes* (courgette flowers dipped in batter and deep fried), *mesclun* (salad leaves including dandelion and hedge-mustard), *daube* (beef stew with wine, cinnamon and lemon peel), *salade Niçoise* (with tuna, egg, black olives and anchovies) and *pain bagnat* (Niçoise salad inside a loaf of bread!).

The Riviera is a region of olive groves. The local black or green olives make tasty *tapenades* (olive pastes with capers and anchovies), delicious served on crusty bread with sun-dried tomatoes. Other local delicacies include truffles, lavender-scented honey and a medley of tasty mountain cheeses. Near the coast, fish dishes reign supreme. Expect to pay at least F250 for a *bouillabaisse*, or else try *bourride* – poor man's fish soup! *Moules frites* (mussels with french fries) are always good value, and don't be surprised if you are presented with a plate of shiny, black, seaweed-draped *oursin* (sea urchins) as they are considered a great delicacy. Simply

A salade Niçoise – no two versions are the same

scrape out the rosy-pink insides and eat them raw with a glass of chilled white wine.

Cuisine Niçoise

The Nice area has developed its own distinctive 'Nissart' cuisine within the Provençal tradition. It reflects the town's former association with Italy, with dishes that seductively blend the best of French and Italian traditions. Indeed, pizzas and pastas taste every bit as good in Menton and Nice as they do over the border, and you have never really had ravioli until you try a plateful in Nice, where the dish was first invented. Look out also for *pissaladière* (olive and onion pizza), *socca* (thin pancakes made of chickpea flour), *petits farcis* (savoury stuffed artichoke hearts, courgettes and tomatoes) and *estocaficada* (stockfish stew).

Local Wines

Eleven per cent of France's wine comes from Provence. The chalky soil and warm, dry, Mediterranean climate lend themselves to the development of smooth, easy-to-drink wines such as Côtes de Provence, known mainly for its dry, fruity, rosé wines. For the adventurous wine drinker there are several wines in the AOC (Appellation d'Origine Contrôlée) category, which come mainly from areas just to the west of the Riviera, but which can readily be found on restaurant wine lists. Particularly sought-after (and not usually cheap) wines include the vigorous red Bandol, the dry white Cassis, and reds, rosés and whites from Palette. The tiny wine region of Bellet near Nice produces some particularly fragrant and full-bodied reds, whites and rosés. The locals swear these wines are the best accompaniments to regional dishes, but few bottles ever get beyond the cellars of the Riviera's most exclusive restaurants.

Gathering the grapes at Bellet

Sweetmeats

For those with a sweet tooth, this sunny region produces plenty of juicy, fragrant fruits, including figs, cherries, melons, pears, strawberries and peaches. Other treats include *pain d'épice* (spiced bread), delicious *marrons glacés* from Collobrières, tempting nougat from St-Tropez, and crystalised flowers and caramelised figs from Grasse.

From Vence to Grasse

Distance
44km

Time
1½ hours; half day with visits

Start point
Vence
➕ 57C4

End point
Grasse
➕ 57A3

Lunch
Taverne Provençale,
Gourdon (£)
✉ place de l'Église
☎ 04 93 09 68 22

Admire the spectacular views from the terraces of Gourdon

Exit Vence on the D2210 signposted Grasse and Tourrettes-sur-Loup. After 3km, just off the road, is Château Notre-Dame-des-Fleurs.

This magnificent 19th-century castle became a contemporary art foundation in 1993 and contains a permanent collection of works by Matisse, Dufy and Chagall.

Continue along the D2210 to Tourrettes-sur-Loup.

Tourrettes is popular with artists and artisans but perhaps best known for its production of violets.

Eight kilometres further on, you will arrive at Pont-du-Loup. From here it is worth taking a short detour to le Bar-sur-Loup.

Clinging to the hillside, this pretty village is surrounded by sweetly scented terraces of jasmine, roses and violets.

Return to Pont-du-Loup; follow signs to Gorges du Loup (D6) and Gourdon.

A tortuous route winds gently up this spectacular gorge, through narrow twists of rock, below precipitous chalky cliffs and past bubbling springs, gushing rapids and sparkling waterfalls.

After 7km, turn left at Bramafan bridge on to the D3 to Gourdon.

Of all the region's perched villages, Gourdon is a veritable eagle's nest, clinging to the summit of a cliff, 500m above the Loup. Visitors crowd its cobbled streets, its gift shops, perfumeries and medieval castle, and admire the breathtaking panorama of the entire Riviera.

The D3 descends gradually towards Grasse via Châteauneuf Pré-du-Lac. Take the first exit at the roundabout on to the D2085 which leads to the heart of Grasse.

Detail on a colourful church façade in Vence's delightful old town

TOURRETTES-SUR-LOUP ✪✪

This pleasant 15th-century town is known as the 'town of violets'. The best time to visit is in March for the Fête des Violettes, when the rose-pink façades of the houses are smothered in tiny purple bouquets. They are later distilled in the regional perfume houses, crystallised or sold in bouquets throughout France. Tourrettes-sur-Loup is also known for its many quality craft shops.

🖪 57B4
ℹ️ 11 avenue Saint-Roch
☎ 04 93 12 34 50
↔ Antibes (➤ 48), Biot (➤ 50), Grasse (➤ 60), Mougins (➤ 76), Villeneuve-Loubet (➤ 90)

VENCE ✪✪

Once the Roman forum of Vintium, this delightful old town became a bishopric in the Middle Ages, and its 10th-century cathedral is the smallest in France. Its interior is rich in treasures, with Roman tombstones embedded in the walls and a remarkable Chagall mosaic.

Artists and writers have long been attracted to the town, just 10km from the crowded coast – including Gide, Valéry, Dufy and D H Lawrence. In 1941 Henri Matisse moved here, but soon fell seriously ill. Dominican sisters nursed him back to health and, in gratitude, he built and decorated the beautiful **Chapelle du Rosaire** for them. The interior is compelling in its simplicity, with powerful black line-drawings of the Stations of the Cross on white faïence, coloured only by pools of yellow, blue and green light from the enormous stained-glass windows. Matisse worked on this masterpiece well into his 80s, considering it his 'ultimate goal, the culmination of an intense, sincere and difficult endeavour'.

🖪 57C4
ℹ️ place du Grand-Jardin
☎ 04 93 58 06 38
↔ Cagnes (➤ 52), St-Paul-de-Vence (➤ 78)

Chapelle du Rosaire
✉️ avenue Henri Matisse
☎ 04 93 58 03 26
🕐 Dec–Oct, Tue and Thu 10–12, 3–5.
♿ Good
💶 Expensive

Above: luxury villas adorn the bay of Villefranche

VILLEFRANCHE ✪

Villefranche remains surprisingly unspoilt, considering its proximity to Nice and Monte-Carlo. Indeed, it has changed little since it was founded in the 14th century as a customs-free port (hence its name). Its beautiful deep bay is fringed with red and orange Italianate houses, atmospheric waterfront bars, cafés and restaurants.

A cobweb of steep stairways and cavernous passageways climb from the harbour through the old town. The narrow, vaulted rue Obscure has sheltered the inhabitants of Villefranche from bombardments throughout history right up to World War II.

The sturdy 16th-century citadel on the waterfront contains galleries of paintings and sculptures by local artists, including Picasso and Miró. On the quay, the 14th-century **Chapelle St-Pierre**, once used to store fishing nets, was decorated in 1957 with frescoes by Villefranche's most famous resident, Jean Cocteau.

VILLENEUVE-LOUBET ✪

Villeneuve-Loubet is dominated by a 33m-high pentagonal watchtower, part of an impressive medieval fortress given to the Villeneuves in 1200 by the Count of Provence. Its **Musée Militaire** has fascinating displays devoted to 20th-century conflicts.

The village's main attraction, however, is the **Musée de l'Art Culinaire**, created in the home of Auguste Escoffier (1847–1935), the great French 'chef of kings and the king of chefs' who invented the *bombe Néro* and *pêche Melba* among other dishes. The museum contains all the things one would expect to find in the world's most famous kitchen, including mouth-watering displays of exquisite sugar, chocolate and marzipan work, which still look good enough to eat.

Where To...

Above: *people-watching in 'St-Trop'*
Below: Santons *dolls – sold as souvenirs
in Gourdon*

Nice

Prices

£   = under F150
££   = F150–F300
£££   = over F300

Opening Times

The restaurants listed here are open for lunch and dinner daily unless otherwise stated. Opening hours change frequently and many restaurants and hotels take an annual holiday in winter. It is always best to telephone before setting out.

Nice's Top Chef

Irresistible local dishes such as *pâté au pistou* and *tripes Niçoise* are the trademarks of Dominic Le Stanc, until recently chef of the Hôtel Négresco's famous Chantecler restaurant, and a name synonymous with the very best in Provençal cuisine. Now all eyes are on La Mérenda, newly acquired by Le Stanc – a tiny, rustic restaurant already popular among Niçoise gourmets.

L'Acchiardo (£)

One of the few authentic café bar/restaurants remaining in old Nice, serving simple, nourishing dishes at reasonable prices, and probably the best *soupe de poissons* in Nice.

✉ 38 rue Droite ☎ 04 93 85 51 16 🕐 Closed Sat eve and Sun 🚌 All buses

Auberge des Arts (££)

The imaginative culinary creations of young chef David Faure are a seductive blend of classic French and 'Nissart' cuisine. His delectable desserts would grace any modern art gallery.

✉ 9 rue Pairolière ☎ 04 93 85 63 53 🕐 Closed Sun, Mon and Aug 🚌 All buses

Auberge de Théo (£)

This friendly trattoria-style restaurant in Cimiez serves delicious pizzas and copious salads.

✉ 52 av Cap de Croix ☎ 04 93 81 26 19 🕐 Closed Sun eve and Mon, 20 Aug–1 Sep 🚌 15, 25

Au Moulin à Fromages (£)

With an imaginative menu of cheese dishes, this rustic restaurant at the heart of the old town offers a change from *la cuisine Provençale*. Try prawns with mascarpone or a camembert *raclette*.

✉ 5 rue à Moulin ☎ 04 93 92 59 00 🕐 Closed Mon lunch 🚌 All buses

Le Chantecler (£££)

Nice's leading restaurant – a bastion of French gastronomy and a truly memorable dining experience. For lunch, the *Menu Plaisir* is very reasonable or, for a really

special occasion, the *Menu Dégustation* is a must.

✉ Hôtel Négresco, 37 promenade des Anglais ☎ 04 93 16 64 00 🕐 Daily 12:30–2:30, 7:30–10:30 🚌 6, 7, 9, 10, 12, airport bus

Le Comptoir (££)

Classical cuisine in a chic turn-of-the-century brasserie, decorated with art-deco panelling, mirrors and lights, and currently very 'in'.

✉ 20 rue St-François-de-Paule ☎ 04 93 92 08 80 🕐 Closed Sat lunch and Sun 🚌 All buses

La Criée (££)

One of the best restaurants in Cours Saleya, especially popular for seafood, oysters and shellfish platters. The three-course *menu navigateur* is excellent value.

✉ 22 cours Saleya ☎ 04 93 85 49 99 🚌 All buses

L'Estocaficada (££)

The regional dishes in this atmospheric bistro are made from ingredients straight from the nearby market, and are ideal for a snack or a full-blown meal, washed down with a reasonably priced Provençal wine.

✉ 2 rue de l'Hôtel de Ville ☎ 04 93 80 21 64 🕐 Closed Sun eve and Mon, except for bookings 🚌 All buses

L'Estrilha (££)

A popular restaurant in the old town and a must for ravioli fans, with a wide choice of sauces. Try *petites fritures* or *paella* to follow, cooked in a huge earthenware pot.

✉ 13 rue de l'Abbaye, Vieille Ville ☎ 04 93 62 62 00 🚌 All buses

Fenocchio (£)

The best ice-cream on the Côte d'Azur.

✉ place Rossetti ☎ 04 93 72 52 🕐 May–Sep 9–12:30AM Rest of year 9AM–midnight Closed Wed 🚌 All buses

Flo (££)

Brasserie-style restaurant in a converted art-deco theatre with the kitchen in full view on the stage! Special late-night menu up to half-past midnight.

✉ 4 rue Sacha Guitry ☎ 04 93 13 38 38 🚌 1, 2, 4, 5, 9, 10, 14, 22, 23, 24

Le Grand Café du Turin (££)

This cosy café serves Nice's best shellfish. Order oysters by the dozen, *coquillages* by the kilo or, if you're feeling really brave, a plateful of sea urchins (*oursins*).

✉ place Garibaldi ☎ 04 93 62 29 52 🕐 Closed Jun 🚌 3, 7, 9, 10, 14

Le Grand Pavois (£££)

Sea bream marinated in Marc de Provence liqueur and flamed over fennel, and langoustines in a rich garlic butter sauce spiked with cognac are just two of the many flavoursome dishes at Nice's top fish restaurant behind the old port.

✉ 11 rue Meyerbeer ☎ 04 93 88 77 42 🕐 12–2:30, 7–10 🚌 9, 10, 14, 20

Lou Pilha Leva (£)

Niçoise fast-food (▶ panel).

✉ 10 rue du Collet ☎ 04 93 13 99 08 🕐 10–10 (midnight in summer) 🚌 All buses

La Mérenda (££)

Irresistible menu of 'Nissart' specialities lovingly prepared by one of France's outstanding chefs (▶ panel).

✉ 4 rue de la Terrace ☎ No phone 🕐 Closed weekends and hols 🚌 All buses ❷ Credit cards not accepted

La Pataterie (£)

It's amazing how many different ways there are to serve potatoes! This cheerful new restaurant with its brightly coloured tablecloths and whitewashed walls is great fun and excellent value.

✉ 53 rue Beaumont ☎ 04 93 89 89 78 🕐 Closed Sun 🚌 3, 7, 20, 35

La Petite Maison (£££)

Local market-fresh dishes near the Opéra. The *hors d'oeuvres Niçoise* is a meal in itself. Book well in advance.

✉ 11 rue St-François-de-Paule ☎ 04 93 92 59 59 🕐 Closed Sun 🚌 All buses

La Rotonde (££)

The Riviera's most original brasserie. A circular restaurant with bright merry-go-round décor, complete with flashing lights, automats and painted wooden horses. The menu is supervised by Alain Llorca, chef of the neighbouring Chantecler restaurant.

✉ Hôtel Négresco, 37 promenade des Anglais ☎ 04 93 16 64 00 🕐 7AM–midnight 🚌 6, 7, 9, 10, 12, airport bus

Le Transsiberien (££)

An epic culinary journey of authentic bortsch and blinis in a great Trans-Siberian rail-carriage.

✉ 1 rue Bottero ☎ 04 93 96 49 05 🕐 Closed Sun eve and Mon 🚌 7, 23, 24

Lou Pilha Leva

'Lou Pilha Leva' in local 'Nissart' patois means 'you take away'. At the heart of old Nice, this hole-in-the-wall serves piping hot plates of *socca*, *pissaladière*, *beignets*, *farcis*, pizza and other Niçoise specialities. Ideal for a snack lunch, with large trestle tables that provide the perfect opportunity to chat to the locals.

The Riviera

Fish Dishes

The world-famous fish soup, *bouillabaisse*, originated here as a nourishing family meal, made with up to a dozen different kinds of fish in a rich stock and served with croûtons smeared with *rouille* (garlicky mayonnaise). *Moules* (mussel dishes) are also delicious and always good value. *Bon appetit!*

Antibes

Le Bacon (£££)

One of the coast's best fish restaurants with exceptional views over old Antibes and unforgettable *bouillabaisse*.

✉ boulevard Bacon, Cap d'Antibes ☎ 04 93 61 65 19 🕐 Closed Mon (except Jul, Aug) and Nov–Jan

Biot

Auberge du Jarrier (££)

Imaginative cuisine and an unmistakably Provençal flavour in an old jar factory.

✉ 30 pass de la Bourgade ☎ 04 93 65 11 68 🕐 Closed Wed eve

Bormes-les-Mimosas

L'Escondudo (££)

Enjoy wholesome regional dishes, flavoured with herbs from the surrounding hills, on a sunny terrace overflowing with bougainvillaea, hidden in a steep back alley.

✉ 4 ruelle du Moulin ☎ 04 94 71 15 53 🕐 Closed Sat and Sun out of season

Le Jardin de Perlefleurs (£££)

It is difficult to better Guy Gedda's exquisite *soupe au pistou*, rabbit quiche and Provençal *daube* in Bormes' top eaterie.

✉ 100 chemin de l'Orangerie ☎ 04 94 64 99 23 🕐 Eve only. Closed Mon

Cannes

Le Croco (£)

Be sure to try the speciality – barbecued fish and meat *brochettes* (kebabs), followed by *crème brûlée* – in this popular, friendly bistro.

✉ 11 rue Louis-Blanc ☎ 04 93 68 60 55 🕐 Closed Sun

L'Espadon (£)

A cheap, cheerful no-frills fish restaurant by the old port – a perfect refuge from the glitz and glamour of Cannes. Delicious paella.

✉ 9 quai St Pierre ☎ No phone

La Palme d'Or (£££)

Join the stars at Cannes' most prestigious restaurant to experience the latest culinary creations of prize-winning master chef Christian Willer.

✉ Hôtel Martinez ☎ 04 92 98 74 14 🕐 Closed Mon and Tue out of season

Cogolin

Port-Diffa (££)

One of the Riviera's top Moroccan restaurants.

✉ Le pont sur la Giscle (RN98 – la Foux) ☎ 04 94 56 29 07 🕐 Mar–Jan. Closed Mon

Collobrières

La Petite Fontaine (£)

Try some regional delicacies of the Massif des Maures on a shady terrace, washed down with wine from the local co-operative.

✉ 1 place de la République ☎ 04 94 48 00 12 🕐 Closed Sun eve and Mon

Èze

La Bergerie (££)

Traditional dishes with a good choice of Côtes de Provence wines. Dine in winter by the open fire, and in summer on the shady terrace overlooking the sea.

✉ RN7, Èze ☎ 04 93 41 03 67 🕐 Closed Mon–Wed eve

Le Cactus (£)

This delightful, vaulted restaurant in Èze's old

gateway serves cheap but tasty *crêpes* (pancakes).

✉ **La Placette, entrée Vieux Village** ☎ 04 93 41 19 02 🕓 10–10 Mar–Oct; in winter, weekends and school holidays only

La Chèvre d'Or (£££)
Inspiring French cuisine in a magnificent medieval castle-hotel with breathtaking sea views to match.
✉ **3 rue du Barri** ☎ 04 92 10 66 66 🕓 Closed mid-Nov to Feb

Fayence
Le Castelleras (£££)
A dish of frogs' legs wrapped in pastry with cream and chives is just one of many local specialities served in this old stone farmhouse.
✉ **route de Seillans** ☎ 04 94 76 13 80 🕓 Closed Wed

Le France (££)
Classic French candle-lit restaurant in the centre of town with a pretty, flower-filled terrace. Start with *terrine de chèvre*, then *magret de canard* followed by *crème brûlée*.
✉ **1 grande rue du Château** ☎ 04 94 76 00 14 🕓 Closed Sun eve and Mon

Fréjus
Brasserie des Arènes (£)
An unlikely-looking café near the Arena, serving tasty, filling portions of *entrecôte frites* or *moules frites*.
✉ **rondpoint les Arènes** ☎ 04 94 51 41 55

Fréjus-Plage
L'Armorique (£)
If you're worried about your figure, this is the restaurant for you; it specialises in crisp, healthy salads and is just a stone's throw from the beach.
✉ **259 boulevard de la Libération** ☎ 04 94 51 58 38 🕓 Closed Tue

La Flambée (£)
You won't be able to resist the delicious *crêpes*, or the popular pizzeria-grill next door, called La Bocca. Booking is strongly recommended.
✉ **407 boulevard de la Libération** ☎ 04 94 53 78 54

La Moule Joyeuse (£)
Moules (mussels) with lemon, *moules* with mustard, *moules Fréjusienne* with celery, carrots and thyme, *moules aphrodisiaque* with ginger and mushrooms, *moules* with everything.
✉ **boulevard de la Libération** ☎ 04 94 44 25 13

La Garde-Freinet
Auberge Sarrasin (££)
This cosy, intimate restaurant at the heart of the Massif des Maures provides the perfect venue to taste *cassoulet Provençal* (a hotpot of white beans, pork and white wine), served by the log fire in winter.
✉ **D558, Massif des Maures** ☎ 04 94 43 67 16 🕓 Closed Mon

Gorbio
Auberge du Village (£)
Delightful village restaurant in Gorbio's main square, serving such delights as stuffed aubergines, seafood salads and courgette flowers.
✉ **8 rue Gambetta** ☎ 04 93 35 87 83 🕓 Closed Mon

Gourdon
Taverne Provençale (£)
Relax over a tasty, light lunch on the terrace here, whilst admiring the grandiose views across the Loup valley to the sea, with Antibes and Cap Roux in the distance.
✉ **place de l'Église** ☎ 04 93 09 68 22

Grasse
Maître Boscq (££)
A must for those who like to try local delicacies. Look out

Provençal Wines
Tobias Smollett once wrote that 'the local wine-merchants brew a balderdash, and even mix it with pigeon's dung and quick-lime'. That was, admittedly, over 200 years ago, but to avoid choosing such unpalatable 'plonk', make sure the bottle is labelled with a quality-controlled AOC (Appellation d'Origine Contrôlée), meaning that the wine is made from recognised varieties of grapes and comes from a certain defined area. Some of the best local wines come from Bellet (► 109 panel), Bandol, Cassis and Palette.

95

Christmas Puddings

Christmas on the Riviera is a time of great gastronomic importance, when families get together for a special meal called *Le Réveillon* on Christmas Eve. It usually starts with oysters or *foie gras*, followed by fish, accompanied by champagne. The best part of the meal is undoubtedly *dessert* – with 13 different puddings, including dried fruits, nuts and nougat, cream cakes, clementines, and not forgetting the *pièce de résistance*, a *Bûche de Noël* (Yule Log).

for *tripes à la mode de Grasse* and the nourishing Grassois cabbage *sous fassoun*, stuffed with pig's liver, sausage, bacon, beans and rice.

✉ **13 rue de la Fontette** ☎ **04 93 36 45 76**

Grimaud
Les Santons (££)

Classic cuisine and impecc-able service in elegant Provençal surroundings. One of the region's top restaurants.

✉ **route Nationale** ☎ **04 94 43 21 02** 🕓 **Closed Wed and Nov–mid-Mar**

Haut-de-Cagnes
Côte Café (£)

Small, café-style restaurant specialising in dishes from the island of Réunion.

✉ **1 place Grimaldi** ☎ **04 92 13 01 22**

Les Peintres (£££)

Former restaurant of master chef Alain Llorca (▶ 93). Smart blue chairs, crisp white linens and splashy modern artwork set the scene for a memorable feast of bold, sun-drenched Mediterranean dishes.

✉ **71 montée de la Bourgade** ☎ **04 93 20 83 08** 🕓 **Closed Wed eve**

Les Issambres
Villa Saint-Elme (£££)

One of the coast's most spectacular restaurant terraces, with exceptional cuisine to match. Try lobster tart for starters, followed by *pigeon en croûte*.

✉ **Hôtel Villa Saint-Elme, corniche des Issambres** ☎ **04 94 49 52 52** 🕓 **Closed Wed (Oct–Jan) and Jan–end Mar**

Juan-les-Pins
La Bodega (£)

A jolly, family restaurant specialising in wood-fire pizzas, pasta and grills,

served with a smile; live music most evenings.

✉ **rue Dautheville** ☎ **04 93 61 07 52**

Café de la Plage (£)

Surely the biggest ice-creams on the Riviera. Try the aptly named Coupe Mont Blanc or Coupe de la Plage with nougat, honey and pralines. Delicious!

✉ **1 boulevard Baudoin** ☎ **04 93 61 37 61**

L'Oasis (££)

Dine on the beach, with stunning views from the Cap d'Antibes to the Îles de Lérins.

✉ **boulevard Charles Guillaumont** ☎ **04 93 61 45 15** 🕓 **Closed eve in winter**

Menton
Don Cicco (£)

Italian cuisine less than a kilometre from the Italian border.

✉ **11 rue St-Michel** ☎ **04 93 57 92 92** 🕓 **Closed Wed**

Le Nautic (££)

Located on the waterfront and highly recommended for fish-lovers. The menu changes according to the daily catch from the nearby fish market.

✉ **1 quai de Monléon** ☎ **04 93 30 03 47**

L'Olivier (££)

This cosy restaurant at the foot of the old town serves giant pizzas from an open oven along with mouth-watering *moules frites* or beef *carpaccio à discretion*.

✉ **21 place du Cap** ☎ **04 93 35 45 65** 🕓 **Closed lunch**

Au Pistou (££)

Regional and Mentonnaise specialities beside the old fishing harbour.

✉ **9 quai Gordon Bennett** ☎ **04 93 57 45 89** 🕓 **Closed Sun eve, Mon and winter months**

WHERE TO EAT & DRINK

Miramar
La Marine (££)
Possibly the best sardines on the Corniche d'Or, on a breezy terrace overhanging the Mediterranean.
✉ port de Miramar ☎ No telephone ⏰ Closed out of season

Monaco
Le Castelroc (££)
This crowded and popular lunch spot opposite the Prince's palace has been run by the same family for over 50 years. They have recently won a local award for exceptional Monégasque cuisine.
✉ place du Palais, Monaco-Ville ☎ 377/93 30 36 68 ⏰ Lunch only. Closed Sat, 1 Dec–20 Jan

Louis XV (£££)
Should you break the bank at the Casino, come to the Louis XV to blow your winnings. The lunch menu is excellent value.
✉ Hôtel de Paris, place du Casino, Monte-Carlo ☎ 377/92 16 30 01 ⏰ Closed Tue, Wed lunch, 1–27 Dec and 17 Feb–4 Mar

La Maison du Caviar (££)
This simple yet smart restaurant serves copious quantities of caviar, blinis, salmon and vodka – redolent of the days of the Tsar.
✉ 1 avenue St-Charles, Monte-Carlo ☎ 377/93 30 80 06 ⏰ Closed Mon eve and Tue, 28 Jun–14 Jul

Polpetta (££)
Hidden away from the clamour of central Monte-Carlo, this vivacious Italian restaurant nonetheless attracts jet-setters and celebrities for a taste of *la dolce vita*.
✉ 2 rue Paradis, Monte-Carlo ☎ 377/93 50 67 84 ⏰ Closed Wed, Sat lunch, 15–30 Oct and 3 Feb–23 Mar

Le Texan (££)
Rub shoulders here with the likes of Crown Prince Albert and Boris Becker over fajitas, enchiladas, burritos and cheap beers at this lively Tex-Mex bar-cum-restaurant.
✉ 4 rue Suffren-Reymond, la Condamine ☎ 377/93 30 34 54 ⏰ Closed Tue

Mougins
Le Moulin de Mougins (£££)
World-famous chef Roger Vergé invented the phrase 'cuisine of the sun' to describe his *nouvelle* Provençal cookery.
✉ Notre-Dame-de-Vie ☎ 04 93 75 78 24 ⏰ Closed Mon, Thu lunch and 11 Feb–11 Mar

Relais à Mougins (£££)
Another of Mougin's gastronomic bastions. Master chef André Surmain is well known for his seasonal cuisine.
✉ place de la Mairie ☎ 04 93 90 03 47 ⏰ Closed Tue lunch and Mon except Jul and Aug

Roquebrune-Village
Le Grand Inquisiteur (£££)
These cave-like, vaulted dining-rooms were once used to shelter livestock. Today they make the perfect setting for a candle-lit dinner *à deux*.
✉ rue du Château ☎ 04 93 28 99 00 ⏰ Closed Thu, Fri lunch, mid-Nov to mid-Dec

La Grotte (£)
Feeling peckish? Then tuck into the *plat du jour* at 'the Cave', a popular troglodyte restaurant at the entrance to the village, with tables spilling out into the square.
✉ place des Deux-Frères ☎ 04 93 35 00 04

Ste-Agnès
La Vieille Auberge (£)
This simple, family-run restaurant on the outskirts of the village is famous for

---

Pastis
The most popular apéritif of the region is pastis, the ubiquitous drink that has come to epitomise the essence of the south in countless classic films and advertisements. This clear aniseed-based liquid has an alcoholic strength similar to that of whisky, and is usually drunk diluted with water and ice, which makes it go white and cloudy. Some brands are drier than others, and some taste strongly of liquorice. Pastis-based cocktails can include grenadine and/or peppermint.

What's 'In' in St-Tropez

Tips on where to be seen and when during your stay in St-Tropez.... For breakfast, Sénéquier's Salon de Thé (✉ quai de Suffren) is a must. *Boules* is on the lunchtime menu at Café des Arts, place des Lices' number one address. L'Échalotte (✉ 35 rue Allard) is currently 'in' for dinner, and the notorious Tropezien institution, Le Gorille (✉ quai de Suffren) remains the place to eat *steak tartare* after the nightclubs close at dawn.

its generous portions of *charcuterie de montagne* and *lapin aux herbes de Provence*.
✉ **Ste-Agnès** ☎ **04 93 35 92 02** ⏰ **Closed Wed**

St-Paul-de-Vence

Chez Andreas (£)

A cheerful café-bar on the village ramparts, ideal for a light lunch or a glass of wine as the sun goes down. Be sure to sample the delectable desserts.
✉ **rempart Ouest** ☎ **04 93 32 98 32**

Le Mas d'Artigny (£££)

Set in beautiful parkland and part of an exquisite 'Relais et Château' hotel, this gourmet restaurant serves exceptional fish dishes.
✉ **route de la Colle** ☎ **04 93 32 95 36**

St-Tropez

Le Bar à Vin (££)

A cosy bistro, hidden in a quiet back street and highly recommended by locals.
✉ **13 rue des Feniers** ☎ **04 94 97 46 10** ⏰ **Eve only. Closed 7 Jan–15 Feb, Wed until 15 Apr**

La Bouillabaisse (££)

A speciality fish restaurant in an ancient fisherman's cottage on the beach.
✉ **plage de la Bouillabaisse** ☎ **04 94 97 54 00** ⏰ **Closed mid-Jan to mid-Feb, mid-Nov to mid-Dec**

La Brasserie Asiatique (££)

The exotic oriental dishes here make a pleasant change from Provençal cuisine.
✉ **Résidence du Port** ☎ **04 94 97 84 82**

Café des Arts (££)

This has been the favourite haunt of the see-and-be-seen

brigade since the sixties. You come for the fun, not the food.
✉ **place des Lices** ☎ **04 97 02 25** ⏰ **Closed Oct–Mar**

La Citadelle (££)

This tiny atmospheric restaurant overflows on to the street. Don't miss the scrumptious *tarte tatin*.
✉ **22 bis rue de la Citadelle** ☎ **04 94 54 81 19** ⏰ **Apr to mid-Oct dinner only. Also lunch from Apr to mid-Jun**

Sénéquier (££)

You can't miss the distinctive red awnings on the waterfront, for this is one of the best-known spots in St-Tropez and a must for breakfast.
✉ **quai Suffren** ☎ **04 94 97 08 98**

Vien Dong (££)

The food here is an excellent *mélange* of Vietnamese, Chinese and Thai, but the main attraction is that the restaurant is owned by a former Mr Universe.
✉ **avenue Paul Roussel** ☎ **04 94 97 09 78**

Valbonne

Auberge Provençale (£)

Enjoy simple, typical country fare in a rustic setting overlooking the ancient arcaded main square.
✉ **place des Arcades** ☎ **04 93 12 29 73**

Villefranche

La Mère Germaine (£££)

One of the most popular waterfront seafood restaurants in Villefranche. Menus change daily depending on the catch.
✉ **quai Courbet** ☎ **04 93 01 71 39**

Nice

Acanthe (£)
This friendly hotel just a stone's throw from Place Masséna is a long-time favourite of budget travellers in Nice. Comfortable and clean. Fifty per cent discount on Plage Galion.
✉ 2 rue Chauvain ☎ 04 93 62 22 44 🚍 All buses

Le Beau Rivage (£££)
Matisse spent two years here and Chekhov, during his stay, wrote *The Seagull* in this elegant art-deco hotel, strategically placed on the waterfront near the opera and the old town.
✉ 24 rue St-François-de-Paule ☎ 04 93 80 80 70 🚍 3, 6, 9, 10, 12, 14

La Belle Meunière (£)
A popular, inexpensive hotel, near the station, with friendly service, private parking and a small garden for breakfast.
✉ 21 avenue Durante ☎ 04 93 88 66 15 🚍 12, 15, 17, 23, 24, 38

Château des Ollières (£££)
Exclusive *belle époque* villa, once owned by a Russian prince (► panel).
✉ 39 avenue des Baumettes ☎ 04 92 15 77 99 🚍 6, 9, 10, 12, 23, 24, 26

Négresco (£££)
World-famous hotel built in the classic wedding-cake style (► 37).
✉ 37 promenade des Anglais ☎ 04 93 16 64 00 🚍 6, 7, 9, 10, 12, airport bus

Palais Maeterlinck (£££)
This villa was once the home of poet Maurice Maeterlinck. Now it is a palatial, modern coastal hotel just four minutes by helicopter from Nice airport, with terraced gardens, a first-class restaurant (Le Mélisande) and a private beach accessed by cable-car.
✉ 30 boulevard Maurice Maeterlinck ☎ 04 92 00 72 00 🚍 14 🚫 Closed early Jan–mid-Mar

La Pérouse (£££)
On the edge of old Nice, this modern hotel with rustic décor enjoys the most painted view of Nice – along the palm tree-lined Baie des Anges. Both Matisse and Dufy stayed here and captured the scene.
✉ 11 quai Rauba-Capéu ☎ 04 93 62 34 63 🚍 38

Le Petit Palais (£££)
Charming *fin de siècle* mansion, once the home of Sacha Guitry. Tranquilly located on the heights of Cimiez, with spectacular views over Nice.
✉ 10 avenue Emile Bieckert ☎ 04 93 62 19 11 🚍 15, 17, 20, 22, 25

Primotel Suisse (££)
An affordable address on the waterfront.
✉ 15 quai Rauba-Capéu ☎ 04 92 17 39 00 🚍 38

Solara (£)
Excellent value in Nice's chic pedestrian zone. Book early.
✉ 7 rue de France ☎ 04 93 88 09 96

Windsor (££)
This eccentric hotel, just five minutes' walk from the sea, features an English-style pub, a Turkish hammam and Thai-style lounges, rooms decorated by local artists and an exotic garden with a lovely palm-fringed pool.
✉ 11 rue Dalpozzo ☎ 04 93 88 59 35 🚍 3, 9, 10, 14

Prices
The following price bands are given on a double room per night basis.

£	up to F350
££	up to F600
£££	over F600

A Russian Romance
The beautiful *belle époque* Château des Ollières, richly furnished and shaded by an acre of garden, is surely one of Nice's most romantic hotels. In the late 19th century, it belonged to Russian Prince Lobanov Rostowsky who, on being called back to Moscow to assume a position in the Russian government, gave it to his mistress as a gift of love. Converted into a luxury hotel in 1990, it still maintains the warm, homely feeling of a private mansion.

The Riviera

Gordon Bennet!

Hôtel La Réserve in Beaulieu-sur-Mer reached the height of its fame in 1887 when millionaire playboy James Gordon Bennet, owner of the *New York Herald*, was cast out from American society following some scandalous behaviour, and moved here to run the Paris edition of his paper from the hotel during the 1880s and 1890s.

Anthéor
Auberge d'Anthéor (££)

A tiny, modern hotel, halfway along the Corniche d'Or. Although there is no beach, there is a small dock for swimming and a pool.

✉ N98, Anthéor ☎ 04 94 44 83 38

Antibes
Auberge Provençale (£)

This traditional-style inn offers friendly service and five cosy, comfortable bedrooms, overlooking the main square of the old town. Booking essential.

✉ 61 place Nationale ☎ 04 93 34 13 24

Beaulieu-sur-Mer
La Réserve (£££)

One of the most exclusive seafront hotels of the Riviera, still with an elegant and formal atmosphere (► panel).

✉ 5 boulevard Maréchal-Leclerc ☎ 04 93 01 00 01

Biot
Galerie des Arcades (£–££)

A characterful 15th-century hotel in a splendid arcaded square, with a restaurant specialising in *spécialités paysannes provençales*.

✉ 14 place des Arcades ☎ 04 93 65 01 05

Bormes-les-Mimosas
Le Bellevue (£)

A simple family-run hotel with spectacular views over red roofs to the sparkling sea beyond.

✉ 12 place Gambetta ☎ 04 94 71 15 15 🕐 Closed winter

Cannes
Martinez (£££)

This deluxe hotel contains Cannes' top restaurant, La Palme d'Or – excellent for star-spotting during the Film Festival.

✉ 73 la Croisette ☎ 04 92 98 73 00

Villa de l'Olivier (££–£££)

A family-run hotel in Cannes' ancient le Suquet district near the beach and the old port, with 24 rooms, swimming pool and garden with views overlooking the roof tops of Cannes. No restaurant.

✉ 5 rue des Tambourinaires ☎ 04 93 39 53 28

Cap d'Antibes
Hôtel du Cap Eden Roc (£££)

'A large, proud, rose-coloured hotel. Deferential palms cool its flushed façade, and before it stretches a ... bright tan prayer rug of a beach.' (F Scott Fitzgerald, *Tender is the Night* ► 101, panel).

✉ boulevard Kennedy ☎ 04 93 61 39 01 🕐 mid-Apr to mid-Oct

Cogolin
Au Coq (££)

This cheerful pink hotel at the bustling heart of Cogolin offers affordable accommodation for those wishing to worship the Tropezienne sun without paying St-Tropez prices.

✉ place de la République ☎ 04 95 54 63 14

Èze
Château Èza (£££)

Former home to Prince William of Sweden, these stunning medieval houses have been linked together to form a luxury eyrie.

✉ rue de la Pise ☎ 04 93 41 12 24

Fayence

Moulin de la Camandoule (£££)

Amid vines and olive trees, this converted 15th-century olive mill is hidden in a peaceful setting just outside Fayence. The atmospheric restaurant specialises in authentic Provençal cuisine.

✉ chemin de Notre-Dame-des-Cyprès ☎ 04 94 76 00 84

Les Oliviers (££)

A comfortable hotel set in pretty Varois countryside, with 22 rooms, sunny terrace and garden. No restaurant.

✉ quartier Ferrage, route de Grasse ☎ 04 94 76 13 12

Grasse

Best Western Hôtel des Parfums (££)

Facilities include a swmming pool and jacuzzi, and a special 1½ hour film 'Introduction to Perfume', prior to visiting Grasse's perfume factories. Ask for a room with a view.

✉ boulevard Eugène-Charabot ☎ 04 93 36 10 10

Grimaud

La Palmeraie (££)

Attractive self-catering accommodation in small villas clustered round two swimming pools, just 3km from the beaches of St-Tropez. Excellent facilities include a restaurant, tennis courts, bar, children's playground and cars, bikes and televisions to rent.

✉ quartier La Boal ☎ 04 94 79 08 00

Juan-les-Pins

Garden Beach Hotel (£££)

One of surprisingly few Riviera hotels actually located right on the beach, this smart hotel is a privileged member of the exclusive '*pieds dans l'eau*' (feet in the water) hotel group.

✉ 15–17 boulevard Baudoin, La Pinède ☎ 04 92 93 57 57

Menton

Des Ambassadeurs (£££)

Menton's top hotel boasts all mod cons and a prime location in the centre of town but, surprisingly, no swimming pool.

✉ 3 rue Partouneaux ☎ 04 93 28 75 75

Le Magali (££)

Book well in advance for this pleasant hotel, and ask for a room with a balcony overlooking the fragrant citrus garden.

✉ 10 rue Villarey ☎ 04 93 35 73 78

Le Mondial (£)

This turn-of-the century hotel with fading décor and a jolly cafeteria-style restaurant is excellent value and extremely popular.

✉ 12 rue Partouneaux ☎ 04 92 10 20 66

Monaco

L'Hermitage (£££)

You need a princely sum to stay at this massive *belle époque* palace at the heart of Monte-Carlo, famed for its spectacular glass-domed Winter Garden foyer, its lavish pink-and-gold restaurant and its marble terrace.

✉ square Beaumarchais, Monte-Carlo ☎ 377/92 16 40 00

Hôtel de France (££)

One of the few affordable hotels in the principality –

'Tender is the Night'

Many illustrious guests of the 1920s and 1930s stayed at the palatial *fin de siècle* Hôtel du Cap Eden Roc, including Charlie Chaplin, Ernest Hemingway and notorious American socialites F Scott and Zelda Fitzgerald, who personified the reckless hedonism of the Riviera. The hotel was the inspiration for F Scott Fitzgerald's famous 'autobiographical novel' *Tender is the Night*. Eden Roc is still considered the most beautiful place for a swim on the whole Riviera, with today's guests including Clint Eastwood and Arnold Schwarzenegger.

Hôtel de Paris

Few hotels can claim as grand a clientele as Monte-Carlo's Hôtel de Paris. In the winter season of 1887 alone, its guests included the Emperor and Empress of Austria, the Dowager Empress of Russia, the Queen of Portugal and the Kings of Sweden and Serbia. The financier Sir Basil Zaharoff, one of the legendary few who have 'broken the bank' at the neighbouring Casino, took over the entire hotel for his stays, bringing his retinue of staff as well as china and cutlery. Now no-one feels the need to bring their own chef, as the restaurant is one of the most highly rated in the country; but crowned heads are less obvious and the Hôtel de Paris is exclusive only to those without the means to pay for its superior comforts and services.

cheap and cheerful and near the station.

✉ 6 rue de la Turbie, Monte-Carlo ☎ 377/93 30 24 64

Hôtel de Paris (£££)

Aristocrats and gamblers have frequented Monte-Carlo's most prestigious address for over 100 years. Facilities include a fine swimming pool, garden and a rooftop restaurant (► panel).

✉ place du Casino, Monte-Carlo ☎ 377/92 16 30 00

Mougins
Le Manoir de l'Étang (£££)

An intimate manor house, set in 5ha of parkland on the outskirts of Mougins, with pool and solarium, a classy restaurant and five golf courses near by.

✉ route d'Antibes – Les Bois de Font-Merle ☎ 04 93 90 01 07 ◷ Closed Nov, Jan

Peille
Belvédère (££)

The only hotel in the village, offering five simple rooms with superb mountain views and a popular restaurant specialising in 'Nissart' cuisine.

✉ 9 la sortie du Village ☎ 04 93 79 90 45

Peillon
Auberge de la Madone (££)

This typical auberge has been lovingly decorated with traditional Provençal fabrics and furniture. Balmy evenings are spent under the stars on the restaurant terrace, whilst enjoying the establishments delicious home-cooking.

✉ pl au Village ☎ 04 93 79 91 17 ◷ Closed 20 Oct–20 Dec, 7–24 Jan

Roquebrune
Vista Palace (£££)

Don't be put off by this ugly, modern building, perched on a 300m-high cliff on the Grande Corniche overlooking Monaco, for inside you will find the ultimate in luxury.

✉ Grande Corniche ☎ 04 92 10 40 00

St-Jean-Cap-Ferrat
Grand Hôtel du Cap Ferrat (£££)

Luxurious palace in lush, tropical gardens, amidst some of the world's most expensive real estate.

✉ boulevard Général de Gaulle ☎ 04 93 76 50 50

Hôtel Royal Riviera (£££)

One of the 'leading hotels of the world', with its own helipad, magnificent gardens and popular poolside lunchtime barbecues. There's even a children's programme.

✉ 3 avenue Jean Monnet ☎ 04 93 76 31 00

Clair Logis (££)

This simple villa hotel is set in a large and lush garden, in a quiet street at the heart of the wooded peninsula. Excellent for those who seek the elegance of the Cap without the prices. No restaurant.

✉ avenue Centrale ☎ 04 93 76 04 57

Ste-Maxime
Hôtel Marie-Louise (£)

A charming hotel surrounded by mimosa, oleander and umbrella pines, just a short walk from the sea and well placed to explore the Massif des Maures.

✉ hameau de Guerrevieille ☎ 04 94 96 06 05

St-Paul-de-Vence

Colombe d'Or (£££)

Once a modest 1920s café where Braque, Matisse, Picasso and Léger used to pay for their drinks with canvases. Now a super-deluxe hotel. Book months in advance.

✉ place du Général de Gaulle
☎ 04 93 32 80 02

La Grande Bastide (££–£££)

An 18th-century country house with ten charming Provençal-style rooms and lovely views of St-Paul. Excellent value. No restaurant.

✉ 1350 route de la Colle
☎ 04 93 32 50 30

Le St-Paul (£££)

This romantic old 'Relais et Châteaux' hotel, at the heart of the village, would make a dreamy honeymoon venue.

✉ 86 rue Grande ☎ 04 93 32 65 25

St-Tropez

Byblos (£££)

More like a mini-Mediterranean village than a hotel, with small villas, flower-filled gardens and neat patios clustered around a pool, fitness centre and boutiques. In summer it is the venue for the famous disco Les Caves du Roy (► 115).

✉ avenue Paul Signac ☎ 04 94 56 68 00

Château de la Messardière (£££)

St-Tropez' most luxurious hotel. Truly palatial.

✉ route de Tahiti ☎ 04 94 56 76 00

La Maison Blanche (£££)

Beautiful old town house, boldly decorated in terracotta and white, in the centre of town on the famous Place des Lices.

✉ place des Lices ☎ 04 94 97 52 66

St-Tropez Peninsula

Le Mas de Chastelas (££–£££)

Experience a unique opportunity by staying in this beautiful 18th-century *mas*, surrounded by vineyards (► panel).

✉ quartier Bertaud Belieu, Gassin ☎ 04 94 56 71 71

La Vigne de Ramatuelle (£££)

A chic yet characterful vineyard villa near St-Tropez' famous beaches and nightspots. Each room has its own private terrace.

✉ route des Plages ☎ 04 94 79 12 50 🕐 Closed Nov, Jan

Vence

Château St-Martin (£££)

An attractive set of villas built around a ruined Templar fortress with a heart-shaped swimming pool and facilities for riding, fishing and tennis.

✉ avenue des Templiers
☎ 04 93 58 02 02 🕐 Closed mid-Oct to mid-Apr

Le Relais Cantemerle (££–£££)

Escape from the bustle of the coast to this tranquil oasis in the heart of the Vençoise hills where you are sure to enjoy its duplex rooms, refreshing pool and one of the best restaurants in Vence.

✉ 258 chemin Cantemerle
☎ 04 93 58 08 18 🕐 Closed Nov–Apr. Restaurant closed Oct–May (May, Jun, Sep closed Mon)

Mas de Chastelas

Picture a traditional, pale-pink shuttered farmhouse, smothered in creeper, surrounded by some of the most cherished vineyards of the Côtes de Provence, and converted into an exclusive hideaway just outside St-Tropez. Add to this characterful rooms, beautifully decorated with gay Provençal fabrics, and exceptional regional cuisine – served by the pool in summer, and by a cosy log fire in winter. The guest list includes Depardieu, Belmondo and other French film idols – no wonder it is such perfection!

Provençal Souvenirs & Gifts

Fabrics

Èze
Tibolo
Typical of many shops in Èze, Tibolo is inside a cave. Its splashy Provençal fabrics contrast boldly with the grey stone walls and sloping floor.
✉ **rue du Brec** ☎ **04 92 10 85 45**

Fayence
Fayence Tissu
This colourful fabric shop boasts over 400 different Provençal prints.
✉ **24 place Léon Roux** ☎ **04 94 76 10 61**

Nice
Pierre de Eres
A choice selection of pretty Provençal prints and tableware.
✉ **11 rue du Marché** ☎ **04 93 85 77 02**

St-Tropez
Souleiado
Row upon row of colour-drenched printed fabrics, traditional Provençal clothing and exclusive gifts. Also in St-Paul-de-Vence.
✉ **traverse du Marbrier – angle rue de la Poste** ☎ **04 94 54 86 55**

Flowers & Perfumes

Cannes
Mélonie
Quite simply the most exquisite dried flower arrangements you are ever likely to see.
✉ **80 rue d'Antibes** ☎ **04 93 68 60 60**

Grasse
Parfumerie Fragonard
The very finest perfumes from Provence. Also, interesting guided tours of the factory.
✉ **20 boulevard Fragonard** ☎ **04 93 36 44 65**

Senteur Lavande
Grasse must be one of the best places to buy flowers. This tiny florist specialises in sensational arrangements made from dried flowers grown in the local valleys.
✉ **rue Jean Ossola** ☎ **04 93 36 82 12**

Nice
Parfums Poilpot
Tiny, traditional perfumery with a wide choice of scents from Grasse. Specialities include 'Soleil de Nice' and 'Bouquet de Nice'.
✉ **10 rue St-Gaëtan** ☎ **04 93 85 60 77** 🚌 **All buses**

St-Paul-de-Vence
Herbier de Provence
A pot-pourri of locally made soaps, herbs, perfumes and bath products. *Ça sent la Provence*!
✉ **St-Paul-de-Vence** ☎ **04 93 32 91 51**

Glassware, Pottery & Wood

Biot
Poterie du Vieux Biot
Biot is famed for its pottery and this beautiful old shop with sand on the floor provides a perfect setting to display earthenware pots of every shape and size, overflowing with exquisite silk flowers.
✉ **4 chemin Neuf** ☎ **04 93 65 10 40**

Verrerie de Biot
Traditional bubble-flecked glassware from Provence's

capital of glass-blowing makes an unusual souvenir or gift.

✉ **chemin des Combes** ☎ **04 93 65 03 00**

Èze

L'Herminette Ezasque

Situated within the walls of Èze's old gateway, this little shop is bursting with *santons*, Christmas crib figures and gifts and sculptures made from olive wood.

✉ **1 rue Principale** ☎ **04 93 41 13 59**

Fayence

Dany

Dazzling displays of hand-painted glassware in a tiny atelier, including lamps, bottles, jars and vases.

✉ **1 bis rue du Mitan** ☎ **04 94 76 19 85**

St-Paul-de-Vence

Le Coucou

The witty handmade ceramics here make highly original gifts.

✉ **place de l'Église** ☎ **04 93 32 91 18**

St-Tropez

Pierre Basset

You will be spoilt for choice here as terracotta and enamelled tiles, jars, pots and vases in sunny colours fill the shelves.

✉ **route des Plages** ☎ **04 94 97 75 06**

Vallauris

Madoura Boutique

Considering Vallauris is the 'town of a hundred potters', it is surprising there are not more exclusive showrooms. This one specialises in unique sculptures, vases and

Picasso-style pots.

✉ **avenue du Tapis Vert** ☎ **04 93 64 66 39**

More Gift Ideas

Cannes

Geneviéve Lethu

A delightful gift shop, crammed from floor to ceiling with presents and home decorations.

✉ **6 rue Maréchal Joffre** ☎ **04 93 68 18 19**

Monaco

Marie Dentelle

An Aladdin's cave of feminine gift ideas, brightly coloured local pottery, and beautiful bedlinen, including amazing handmade quilts made in traditional Provençal material.

✉ **10 rue Princesse Caroline, la Condamine** ☎ **377/93 30 43 40**

Viking Yachts Monaco

Decorative items with a nautical theme – to kit out your yacht, perhaps?

✉ **22 boulevard des Moulins, Monte-Carlo** ☎ **377/92 16 16 80**

St-Tropez

La Maison des Lices

An emporium of expensive gifts and designer furniture, with two stores packed with tempting Mediterranean products.

✉ **2 & 18 boulevard Louis Blanc** ☎ **04 94 97 62 15**

Valbonne

Le Petit Canard

This high-quality gift shop is full of novel souvenirs and things you would love to buy but don't really need. A browser's paradise.

✉ **25 place des Arcades** ☎ **04 93 12 93 92**

A Ray of Sunshine

Souleiado is a Provençal word meaning 'a sun-ray piercing through the clouds' and is the name of the leading manufacturer of block-printed Provençal textiles. The company was founded in 1938 by Charles Deméry in a successful attempt to revive a 200 year-old textile industry. Today, the original 18th-century fruitwood blocks still form the basis for all the Souleiado patterns.

Fashion

A Royal Shop

Replay's motto states 'If you can't find it in our store, you don't need it!' and it's true, for in this shop belonging to Princess Stéphanie of Monaco is a vast array of smart, trendy jeans, sweaters, shirts, jackets, shoes and accessories in all the 'in' colours for men, women and children. Next door is the Replay Café, where Stéphanie often goes for a bite to eat in the light, spacious brasserie that prides itself on using only natural, home-grown produce.

Biot
Chacok
Bright colours and bold designs by a local Biot designer.
✉ route de la Mer ☎ 04 93 65 60 60

Juan-les-Pins
Ipsofacto
This small shop on La Pinède sells highly wearable designer fashions by Trussardi, Armani and Jiki (▶ 107, panel).
✉ La Pinède, 17 boulevard Baudoin ☎ 04 93 61 70 01

Legend
Young, trendy designs for the seriously fashionable here include French Connection, Kenzo, Moschino and Caterpillar labels.
✉ boulevard Baudoin, Galerie Eden Beach ☎ 04 93 67 33 55

Naf-Naf
Brightly coloured, sporty fashions for men, women and children.
✉ 11 boulevard Baudoin ☎ 04 93 61 26 97

Patounet
Jazzy swimwear right on the waterfront.
✉ Le Colombier, promenade du Soleil ☎ 04 93 61 16 10

Monaco
Diesel
This popular clothing chain produces casual, affordable clothing for men and women.
✉ 15 rue Grimaldi, la Condamine ☎ 377/93 50 34 14

Floriane
Enchanting children's fashions from 0–14 years. Tiny tots can play on the floor with Babar and Tintin while their parents shop.
✉ 17 avenue des Spélugues, Galerie le Métropole, Monte-Carlo ☎ 377/92 16 09 16

Hermès
The ultimate in French chic. The steep prices in this boutique come with a lofty sea view to match.
✉ 11–15 avenue de Monte-Carlo, Monte-Carlo ☎ 377/93 50 64 89

Karen
A smart boutique amid the trashy tourist shops of Monaco-Ville, selling solely 'Karen', chic Italian prêt-à-porter.
✉ 22 rue Princesse Marie de Lorraine, Monaco-Ville ☎ 377/93 50 31 41

Replay
Princess Stéphanie of Monaco owns this shop (▶ panel).
✉ 57 rue Grimaldi, la Condamine ☎ 377/93 25 30 40

Society Club
Men will love this stylish, macho shop, fitted out with wood and leather, selling the latest in designer labels such as D&G, Boss, Cerrutti and Moschino.
✉ Centre Commercial le Métropole, Monte-Carlo ☎ 377/93 25 25 01

Nice
Durrani
Classic haute couture and exclusive perfumes, created by the King of Afghanistan!
✉ 8 rue Massenet ☎ 04 93 87 26 34

Eva's
Sexy French and Italian underwear by Nina Ricci, La Perla, Lise Charmel and

Marvel. The height of luxury.

✉ **10 rue de la Liberté** ☎ **04 93 16 22 46**

St-Raphaël
Alain Manoukian
Chic, affordable women's clothing by a local Provençal designer. Other boutiques in Monaco, Nice and St-Tropez (► panel).

✉ **6 boulevard Félix Martin**
☎ **04 94 95 00 44**

St-Tropez
Blanc Bleu
Stylish, sporty fashion for both sexes.

✉ **3 rue Allard** ☎ **04 94 97 08 01**

Kid Cool
Shop here for bright, sporty clothing (age 3 months to 12 years) if you want your child to be a 'Cool Kid'. The pyjamas are particularly cute.

✉ **3 rue Gambetta** ☎ **04 94 97 01 78**

Quicksilver Board-Riders Club
Calling all budding surf-boarders … it's no good taking to the water in St-Tropez if you don't have all the latest looks. Come here first to be kitted out!

✉ **33 rue Allard** ☎ **04 94 97 73 22**

Accessories

Cannes
Cravaterie Nazionali
Designer ties.

✉ **79 rue d'Antibes** ☎ **04 93 99 78 88**

Grasse
Monique Maroquinerie
Quality leather handbags, wallets, belts and other accessories in innovative styles and colours by Longchamp, Mulberry and Kipling.

✉ **5 rue Jean Ossola**

Monaco
La Botterie
You'll find all the latest trends in footwear here.

✉ **14 boulevard des Moulins, Monte-Carlo** ☎ **377/93 25 80 55**

Divina
Flamboyant costume jewellery and other accessories by Lacroix (► panel), Kenzo and Dior.

✉ **36 boulevard des Moulins, Monte-Carlo** ☎ **377/93 50 52 47**

Nice
Swatch Store
Check your watch against the very latest timepieces from Swatch.

✉ **10 avenue de Verdun**
☎ **04 93 82 16 17**

St-Paul-de-Vence
Bleu comme là-bas
A wacky, bright orange jewellery shop owned by a young, imaginative designer. Affordable and fun.

✉ **38 rue Grande** ☎ **04 93 32 04 17**

St-Tropez
Rondini
Rondini's famous Roman-gladiator-style *sandales Tropeziennes* were invented in 1927 and sales are still thriving.

✉ **16 rue Georges Clemenceau**
☎ **04 94 97 19 55**

Sunglasses Hut
Anyone who's anyone would not be seen without their sunglasses in St-Tropez!

✉ **1 rue Allard**
☎ **04 94 97 76 63**

Local Talent
Look out for items produced by local Riviera designers: notably bright and bold clothes by Biot resident Arlette Chacok; evening wear by Jiki, a glamorous Monégasque designer; and the smart, affordable daytime separates of Alain Manoukian. The region's top name, however, is undoubtedly Christian Lacroix, one of *haute couture's* most innovative and eclectic designers, famous for his classic yet daring, feminine yet boldly Mediterranean, fashions and accessories.

Food & Drink

Symbol of Provence
The olive tree has long been the symbol of Provence, introduced by the Greeks 3,000 years ago as 'the tree of wisdom, abundance and glory'. Over 50 varieties of olive tree now grow on the Riviera. Harvesting takes place from November (for the ripe green ones) to January (for the more mature black ones). It takes 1,000 kilos of olives to produce 10 to 15 litres of oil.

Cannes
Ceneri
One of France's leading cheese stores with over 300 varieties – from huge rounds of runny brie to tiny *boutons de culotte* (trouser-button) goats' cheese.

✉ **22 rue Meynadier** ☎ **04 93 43 07 70**

Èze
Terre de Provence
A cellar full of local wines from southern France; also choice wines from Bordeaux, Alsace and the Loire, champagne and *foie gras*.

✉ **6 rue Principale** ☎ **04 92 10 85 63**

Fréjus
Le Provençal
An old-fashioned pâtisserie and sweet shop serving local specialities – chocolate chestnuts, *marrons glacés*, *pavés du cloître* ('paving stones' from Fréjus' famous cloisters) and bags of green and black chocolate-coated almonds called *olives de Provence*.

✉ **44 rue Jean Jaurès** ☎ **04 94 51 08 51**

Gassin
Petit Village
The wines of the Maîtres Vignerons of St-Tropez on sale here are considered among the best Côtes de Provence wines.

✉ **La Foux** ☎ **04 94 56 32 04**

Gourdon
Ste-Catherine
Fine *produits de Provence*, all made in and around Gourdon, including 20 different mustards, 25 different vinegars, 50 different jams, and scrumptious spice cake, a village speciality.

✉ **Gourdon** ☎ **04 93 09 68 89**

Menton
DOC D'Italia
No need to cross the border to stock up on Italian goodies. This little store has everything from *panettone* to *pecorino*.

✉ **5 rue Piéta** ☎ **04 93 35 44 29**

Huilerie St-Michel
Classic family-run corner store selling their own olive oil, patés and *tapenades*, and dried fruit and nuts in sacks.

✉ **5 rue de Bréa** ☎ **04 93 35 71 04**

La Hutte Fromagère
Four hundred French cheeses in a small, pungent store, including bite-sized *chèvres*, and an interesting Corsican selection.

✉ **16 place Clemenceau** ☎ **04 93 35 99 00**

La Réserve Mentonnaise
A wide choice of French wines together with a selection of exclusive terrines, mustards, coffees and spices from Fauchon, the famous Parisien delicatessen.

✉ **7 rue Piéta** ☎ **04 93 57 68 93**

Monaco
Les Caves du Grand Échanson
Suppliers of exclusive wines and spirits to Prince Rainier.

✉ **32 boulevard des Moulins, Monte-Carlo** ☎ **377/92 05 61 01**

L'Oenothèque
An old wood-panelled store which stocks fine cognacs, armagnacs and French wines from 1928–97.

✉ Galerie du Sporting, 2 avenue Princesse Alice, Monte-Carlo ☎ 377/93 25 82 66

Richart Design et Chocolat
Sophisticated chocolates – almost too good to eat.
✉ Centre Commercial le Métropole, Monte-Carlo ☎ 377/93 30 15 06

Mougins
Boutique du Moulin
If you can't afford dinner in one of France's top establishments (➤ 97), console yourself with mustard, jam or *tapenade* from chef Roger Vergé's shop.
✉ place du Commandant Lamy ☎ 04 93 90 00 91

Nice
Alziri
This old family shop presses its own olive oil and sells *olives de Nice* by the kilo. A wonderful Niçoise institution.
✉ 14 rue St-François-de-Paule ☎ 04 93 85 76 92 🚌 All buses

Caprioglio
Wine store in old Nice, to suit all purses – from *vin de table* (stored in giant orange tanks) to the top French *crus*.
✉ 16 rue de la Préfecture ☎ 04 93 85 66 57 🚌 All buses

Domaine Massa
Hidden in the steep, sun-soaked hills behind Nice, this old farm cultivates two distinctly Niçoise products – carnations and Bellet wine (➤ panel). Phone in advance for a tasting.
✉ 425 chemin de Crémat, 06200 Nice ☎ 04 93 37 80 02

Espuno
One of France's premier bakeries. Try the regional *fougasse*.

✉ 35 rue Droite ☎ 04 93 80 50 67 🚌 All buses

Maison Auer
Nice's last traditional maker of crystallised fruits, famed throughout France. Apricots, figs, clementines and pears that melt in your mouth.
✉ 7 rue St-François-de-Paule ☎ 04 93 85 77 98 🚌 All buses

Pont du Loup
Confiserie des Gorges du Loup
Taste before you buy the many mouth-watering products made at this traditional jam-making factory.
✉ Pont du Loup ☎ 04 93 59 32 91 ❓ Factory tours available 9–12 and 3–6

St-Raphaël
Nougat Cochet
This regional speciality has been made here for several generations.
✉ 9 boulevard Felix Martin ☎ 04 94 95 01 67

St-Tropez
La Tarte Tropezienne
The tempting display of pâtisseries entices you into this small shop to try *la Tarte Tropezienne* – a light, fluffy cream cake created in 1955 to a secret recipe.
✉ boulevard Louis Blanc ☎ 04 94 97 19 77

Villeneuve-Loubet
L'Univers du Vin
A giant wine warehouse on the main road between Cagnes and Antibes and a great place for bargain wines. You can even order personalised wine labels.
✉ route National 7, Villeneuve-Loubet ☎ 04 93 73 73 94

Wine from Bellet
Nice's tiny AOC wine region called Bellet is little known, largely because the majority of the 1,200 hectolitres produced annually never get beyond the cellars of the Riviera's top restaurants. The special quality of the wines is attributed to their unusual grape varieties and the sea and mountain air. The full-bodied red, with its wild cherry bouquet, can be aged up to 30 years. The golden white is reminiscent of Chablis and the rosé is quite the best accompaniment to local fish specialities.

Art, Antiquities & Books

The Second Nice School

The Riviera is still very much a mecca of modern art thanks largely to the Second School of Nice (the first was during the Renaissance). Starting in the late 1950s as a neo-realist reaction to abstract expressionism, the movement was led by multimedia iconoclasts Klein, Rayasse, César, Arman, Ben and Tinguely (▶ 22). Their extraordinary constructions of consumer junk, smashed machinery and burnt musical instruments were designed as a spoof on society and the precious world of contemporary art.

Antibes
Heidi's English Bookshop
The biggest English bookshop on the Côte d'Azur, with a wide choice of new and used books, stationery and cards.
✉ 24 rue Aubernon ☎ 04 93 34 74 11

Biot
Aquarelle Delaplace
You will always remember your visit if you buy a print, etching or original painting of the Riviera from here.
✉ 27 impasse des Arcades ☎ 04 93 65 50 13

Fayence
Sybille
Local artist Sybille's dynamic landscapes and bold, splashy flower paintings will make unusual presents to take home.
✉ 6 rue de Mitan ☎ 04 94 84 16 88

Fréjus
Riquet Beaux-Arts
A painters' paradise, with supplies of pens, paper, pastels and paints.
✉ 69 rue St-François-de-Paule ☎ 04 94 52 00 19

Grasse
Lècritoire et la Plume
This small shop specialises in beautiful hand-made paper, fountain pens, highly original greetings cards and other exclusive stationery.
✉ rue Marcel Journet ☎ 04 93 40 05 78

Monaco
FNAC
Not only one of Monaco's largest bookstores, but come here also for television, video, hi-fi, camera and computer needs, as well as to order tickets for theatre, opera and concert performances or to have your films developed.
✉ Centre Commercial le Métropole, Monte-Carlo ☎ 377/93 10 81 81

Nice
Atelier Galerie Dury
Contemporary paintings, sculptures and reliefs on a nautical theme by award-winning artist Christian Dury.
✉ 31 rue Droite, Vieille Ville ☎ 04 93 62 50 57 🚌 All buses

Cinnamon
It comes as a surprise to find such a delightfully rustic shop in the middle of a city. Inside is a veritable treasure trove of traditional Provençal antiques, pine and fine furnishings.
✉ 10–12 rue Jules Gilly ☎ 04 93 80 70 72

Galerie Ferrero
Exponents of the Second Nice School – very modern and very expensive. (▶ panel).
✉ 24 rue de France/4 rue du Congrès ☎ 04 93 98 34 44

Tourette J
Antique clocks, watches and musical boxes have been Monsieur Tourette's speciality for over 30 years.
✉ 17 rue Lépante ☎ 04 93 92 92 88

St-Tropez
Aux Beaux Arts
This small gallery, tucked away in a back street of the village, specialises in enchanting watercolours of St-Tropez and the surrounding countryside.
✉ 5 place de l'Ormeau ☎ 04 94 97 87 67

Specialist Shops

Antibes

Antibes Shipservices

Everything nautical from 'boaty' keyrings to fashionable yachting gear.

✉ **112 boulevard Aguillon**
☎ **04 93 34 68 00**

Menton

Coutellerie E Garnero

This 100-year-old shop specialises in the unlikely combination of knives and umbrellas – surely one of the most old-fashioned, eccentric shops on the Riviera.

✉ **8 rue St-Michel** ☎ **04 93 57 03 60**

Monaco

Manufacture de Monaco

A small, exclusive shop which supplies Monaco's royal family with traditional Monégasque porcelain, silverware, crystal and table linen.

✉ **Centre Comerciale le Métropole, 4 avenue de la Madone, Monte-Carlo**
☎ **377/93 50 64 63**

Monaco Models

If you are unable to visit Monaco's famous Grand Prix or the Monte-Carlo Car Rally, come to this extraordinary model shop to view the cars instead (▶ panel).

✉ **3 rue Terrazzani, la Condamine** ☎ **377/93 30 42 33**

Monaquatic-Aquariophile

Feeling inspired after a visit to Monaco's remarkable Musée Océanographique (▶ 24)? Then this specialist aquarium store is the place for you.

✉ **20 avenue Crovetto Frères, la Condamine** ☎ **377/92 16 03 40**

Nice

Arta Photo

Come here for photographic equipment, films and a quality development service.

✉ **8 rue de Nice** ☎ **04 93 887 14 46**

L'Atelier des Jouets

A magical shop full of sturdy, educational toys and games in wood, metal and cloth.

✉ **1 place de l'Ancien Sénat**
☎ **04 93 13 09 60**

Halogene

You will find everything imaginable for a trendy home in this chic, modern interior design shop, including unusual furniture, lighting and gift ideas.

✉ **21/23 rue de la Buffa** ☎ **04 93 88 96 26**

Go Sport

The department store for sports fanatics with sections dedicated to every sport imaginable.

✉ **13 place Masséna** ☎ **04 93 92 34 04**

Nocy-Bé

Ecological, educational gifts from around the world.

✉ **4 & 6 rue Jules Gilly** ☎ **04 93 85 52 25**

Transparence

As the name suggests, everything in this shop is see-through – paper-weights, lampstands, trays, keyrings ...

✉ **2 rue Jules Gilly** ☎ **04 93 13 91 67**

St-Paul-de-Vence

La Maison de Pinocchio

The dolls and puppets in this cramped, cave-like shop will take you back to your childhood.

✉ **La Vieille Echappé**

Mecca of Motor Racing

The first Monte-Carlo Car Rally in 1902 occasioned the world's first tarmac road. The racing has come a long way since then, when 'gentlemen' drivers competed at speeds averaging 25kph. Nowadays, the real crowd-puller is the Monaco Grand Prix during the second week of May, with thousands of spectators wild with suspense on the pavements of the town.

Children's Attractions

Marineland

A wonderful world of performing sea lions, killer whales, dolphins, and close underwater encounters with sharks (safely, within a transparent tunnel!). Children love the 'Jungle des Papillons' with exotic butterflies, huge hairy spiders and other creepy-crawlies. Younger children enjoy the pony tours, face-painting and stroking the animals at 'La Petite Ferme Provençale'. Older children hurtle down the Aqua-Splash water slides and Mum and Dad try their hand at wacky crazy golf. All this and more at Marineland.

Antibes
Antibes Land

All ages enjoy this amusement park – its big wheel, roller-coaster and even its bungee-jumping!

✉ route N7 ☎ 04 93 95 23 03
🕐 Jun 8PM–2AM, Jul–Aug 3:30–2AM; Easter, Wed, Sat, Sun, hols 2–2

Marineland

The greatest marine show in Europe (► panel).

✉ route N7 ☎ 04 93 33 49 49
🕐 Daily 10–6

Cannes
Formule Kart'in

Indoor go-karting circuit for children (aged 6 upwards) and adults, in the heart of Cannes.

✉ 215 avenue Francis Tonner (RN7) ☎ 04 93 47 88 88
🕐 Daily 2–midnight (Sun 2–8)

Gonfaron
Village des Tortues

Children find the one-hour tour of this remarkable 'village' (the world's only tortoise conservation centre), with its 1,200 turtles and tortoises, truly fascinating.

✉ 83590 Gonfaron (off autoroute Aix-Cannes) ☎ 04 94 78 26 41 🕐 Mar–Nov, daily 9–7

Juan-les-Pins
Visiobulle

Discover the underwater world of 'Millionnaires' Bay' in a glass-bottomed boat. Reservation advisable.

✉ embarcadère Courbet ☎ 04 93 67 02 11 🕐 Apr–end Sep, departures at 11, 1:30, 3, 4:30 (also 9:30, 6, and evenings mid-Jun to end Aug)

Monaco
Musée National

Huge collection of dolls, from 18th century to Barbie.

✉ 17 avenue Princesse Grace, Monaco ☎ 377/93 30 91 26
🕐 Oct–Easter 10–12:15, 2:30–6:30; Easter–Sep 10–6:30. Closed 1 Jan, 1 May, 19 Nov, 25 Dec 🚌 4, 6

Les Terrasses de Fontvieille

Prince Rainier's collections of model boats and vintage cars, a zoo and even a MacDonalds!

✉ terrasses de Fontvieille ☎ Zoo 377/93 25 18 31; naval museum 377/92 05 28 48; classic car exhibition 377/92 05 28 56
🕐 Tel for details 🚌 5, 6

Mougins
Musée de l'Automobile

Older children in particular enjoy visiting the unique, radiator-shaped Car Museum, viewing footage of classic races and testing out the Buggy Cross go-cart circuit.

✉ 772 chemin de Font-de-Currault (just off autoroute A8 Nice-Cannes, exit Les Hautes Bréguires) ☎ 04 93 69 27 80
🕐 Museum daily 10–7; Buggy Cross Jul, Aug 10–7, Sep–Jun weekends only

Nice
Musée des Trains Miniatures

A fascinating railroad museum. Children large and small love it.

✉ avenue Impératrice Eugénie ☎ 04 93 97 41 40 🕐 winter 9:30–5, summer 9:30–7
🚌 bus 22

Port-Grimaud
Luna Park

Exhilarating fairground rides.

✉ Golfe de St-Tropez ☎ 04 94 56 35 64 🕐 Apr–late Jun 8:30PM–1AM; late Jun–mid-Sep 8:30PM–2AM; Sun and hols from 4PM

Participatory Sports

Ballooning

Association Aérostatique Côte d'Azur

Don't forget your camera for a chance-of-a-lifetime flight along the coast in a hot-air balloon (from F1,200 per person).

✉ chemin de la Tour de St-Roman de Bellet, Nice ☎ 04 93 37 97 72

Fishing

Guiguot Marine, Antibes

Tired of lazing on the beach? Book a day trip deep-sea fishing.

✉ 11 avenue Novembre ☎ 04 93 34 17 17 🕐 Jun–Oct

Golf

Golf Club Cannes-Mandelieu

One of the largest golf-courses in Europe.

✉ route du Golf, 06210 Mandelieu-la Napoule ☎ 04 93 49 55 39

Royal Mougins Golf Club

Considered by many the best golf club on the Côte d'Azur.

✉ 424 avenue du Roi ☎ 04 92 92 49 69

Hang-gliding, Paragliding & Ultra-light

Fédération Française de Vol Libre

Surely the ultimate way to view the Riviera.

✉ 4 rue de Suisse, Nice ☎ 04 93 88 62 89

Horse Riding

Popular areas include the Massif de l'Esterel (► 17), the Massif des Maures

(► 64) and the countryside around Grasse.

✉ Association Régionale du Tourisme Équestre Provence-Côte d'Azur ☎ 04 93 42 62 98

Sailing

Centre Nautique Municipal de Cannes

Tuition in sailing dinghies and catamarans, and surf-boarding for adults and children.

✉ 9 rue Esprit Violet ☎ 04 92 18 88 88

Scuba Diving

Centre International de Plongée de Nice

The Riviera offers some of the finest diving in Europe.

✉ 2 ruelle des Moulins 🕐 04 93 55 59 50

Tennis

Lawn Tennis Club Suzanne Lenguen, Nice

Venue of the Nice Open and former club of French tennis star Yannick Noah.

✉ 5 avenue Suzanne Lenguen ☎ 04 93 96 17 70

Monte-Carlo Country Club

Excellent all-round sports club with 23 tennis courts (including five floodlit and two covered), swimming pool, jacuzzi, gym, snooker, squash and bridge.

✉ avenue Princesse Grace ☎ 377/93 41 30 15

Trekking & Rock Climbing

Club Alpine

Rock and ice cascade climbing expeditions.

✉ 13 avenue Isola Bella, Cannes ☎ 04 93 68 46 17

Spectator Sports

The region's number one spectator sport is *le foot* (football) with locals passionately supporting their teams. The Monte-Carlo Car Rally, the Monaco Grand Prix and the Monte-Carlo and Nice Open Tennis Championships are also huge crowd-pullers, along with regular horse-racing at Cagnes. Every summer, crowds flock to Nice for its international triathlon (cycling, running, swimming) – the so-called 'Madman's Promenade'. Fewer people attend the Christmas day skinny-dip, the great Bain de Noël.

Arts &
Entertainment

Café de Paris
This beautifully renovated art-deco triumph contains a restaurant as well as a gaming house, which in its heyday attracted the world's most elite society. Ladies' man Edward VII was a frequent visitor, and the delicious flambéed dessert *crêpe suzette* was created here, named after one of his companions.

Casinos, Cinemas & Night Spots

Antibes
La Siesta
One of the Côte d'Azur's most exotic nightclubs, with open-air dance floors, fountains, flaming torches and a wave-shaped casino.
✉ route du Bord-de-la-Mer (between Antibes and la Brague) ☎ 04 93 33 31 31
🕐 Mid-May to mid-Sep, 11PM–approx 4AM

Cannes
Planet Hollywood
This popular bar, opened in May 1997 by Bruce Willis, Demi Moore, John Travolta and Sylvester Stallone, is curently one of the places to see and be seen.
✉ 1 les Allées de la Libérté
☎ 04 93 39 24 53
🕐 11:30–1AM

Juan-les-Pins
Whisky à Gogo
Join the locals for the latest sounds in this overflowingly popular nightclub.
✉ La Pinède ☎ 04 93 61 26 40

Monaco
Café de Paris
Even if you are not a big spender, you will be tempted by the dazzling array of slot-machines in this famous café (▶ panel).
✉ place du Casino, Monte-Carlo ☎ 377/92 16 20 20
🕐 All day from 10AM

Le Casino
The most famous, ritziest casino on the Riviera, but with a F50 entrance fee. Passport required. Jacket and tie recommended (▶ 16).

✉ place du Casino, Monte-Carlo ☎ 377/92 16 21 21
🕐 From 3PM till dawn

Cinema d'Été
An open-air cinema, summertime only.
✉ avenue Princesse Grace, Monte-Carlo ☎ 377/93 25 86 80

Jimmi'z
Join the jet set at the chicest disco on the Riviera.
✉ 26 avenue Princesse Grace, Monte-Carlo ☎ 377/93 16 22 77
🕐 11:30PM–5AM. Closed Mon, Tue and Nov–Easter

The Living Room
Piano bar and disco, in the centre of Monte-Carlo.
✉ 7 avenue des Spélugues, Monte-Carlo ☎ 377/93 50 80 31

Le Sporting
Monaco's main cinema complex, inside an arcade of smart shops, with four screens showing films in their original versions.
✉ place du Casino, Monte-Carlo ☎ 377/93 30 81 08

Nice
L'Ambassade
One of the most beautiful nightclubs on the Riviera.
✉ 18 rue du Congrès ☎ 04 93 88 88 87 🕐 9PM–2:30AM

Casino Ruhl
Nice's glitzy, glamorous casino offers spectacular dinner cabarets as well as private gaming rooms.
✉ promenade des Anglais ☎ 04 93 87 95 87

Cinémathèque
A must for cinephiles … showing original golden oldies as well as all the latest releases.
✉ Acropolis, 3 esplanade

Kennedy ☎ 04 92 04 06 66 🎬 Screenings on Tue, Wed, Thu at 2:30, 5, 8; Fri–Sat 2:30, 5, 8, 10; Sun 3pm 🚌 All buses

La Douche
This tiny, crowded nightclub also contains France's first cyber-café.
✉ 34 cours Saleya ☎ 04 93 62 81 31 🕐 10:30AM–2.30AM 🚌 All buses

L' Iguane
An old-established Niçoise night spot in the old port, enhanced with tropical guerrilla décor. Dance floor for poseurs.
✉ 5 quai des deux Emmanuels ☎ 04 93 56 83 83 🕐 Open daily 🚌 Bus 2, 9, 10

La Suite
A trendy after-dinner venue with sumptuous theatrical baroque décor. The cocktail evenings and fancy-dress theme nights are popular with tourists.
✉ 2 rue Bréa ☎ 04 93 92 92 91 🕐 Mon–Sat 10:30–2:30AM 🚌 All buses

St-Tropez
Les Caves du Roy
St-Tropez' spiciest night spot, in the elegant and exotic Hôtel Byblos.
✉ Hôtel Byblos, avenue Paul Signac ☎ 04 94 56 68 00 🕐 Easter–Oct 11PM–approx 6AM

Theatre, Opera, Classical Music

Menton
Théâtre Français Palermo
Small theatre showing primarily French plays, operettas and recitals.
✉ Palais de l'Europe, avenue Boyer ☎ 04 93 557 57 00

Monaco
Salle Garnier
Monaco's world famous opera house; designed by Charles Garnier, architect of the Paris Opéra (▶ 16). Salle Garnier has played host to many great artists over the years.
✉ place du Casino ☎ 377/92 16 22 99

Nice
L'Acropolis
This vast, modern congress, arts and tourism centre is popular for theatre, films and concerts (▶ panel).
✉ 1 esplanade Kennedy ☎ 04 93 92 83 00 🚌 All buses

Opéra de Nice
Home of the Nice Opera, the Philharmonic Orchestra and Ballet Corps, this rococo extravaganza in red and gold is modelled on the Naples Opera House.
✉ 4/6 rue St-François-de-Paule ☎ 04 92 17 40 40 🚌 All buses

Théâtre de Nice (TDN)
A modern theatre containing two auditoria, and presenting world-class shows.
✉ promenade des Arts ☎ 04 93 80 52 60 🚌 All buses

Ticket Sales

Cannes, Palais des Festivals
✉ Tourist Office, 1 la Croisette ☎ 04 93 39 24 53

Monaco, FNAC
✉ Centre Commercial le Métropole, Monte-Carlo ☎ 377/93 10 81 81

Nice, FNAC
✉ Nice Étoile, 30 avenue Jean Médecin ☎ 04 92 17 77 77

Nice's Acropolis
Love it or hate it, one thing is for sure – you can't ignore this monstrous mass of smoked glass and concrete slabs at the very hub of modern Nice. With its four high-tech auditoria, concert hall, bowling alley, exhibition halls, cinémathèque (▶ 114) and extensive conference facilities, it has been voted 'Europe's best congress centre' for the past three years.

What's On When

Changing Dates
Note that dates may change every year. For complete listings and precise dates of events, pick up a copy of the annual lists, available in most tourist offices.

January
Fête de Ste-Dévote, Monaco
Monte-Carlo Car Rally (end of month)

February
Nice Carnival (two weeks, ➤ 30)
Monte-Carlo International Circus Festival (first week)
Fête du Citron, Menton (10-day festival ➤ 67)
Corso du Mimosa, Bormes-les-Mimosas (10 Feb, ➤ 51)
Olive and Grape Festival, Valbonne (➤ 49)

March
Dance Festival, Cannes
Festin es Courgourdons – festival of dried, sculpted gourds, Nice
Fête des Violettes, Tourrettes-sur-Loup (➤ 88)
Semi Marathon International de Nice

April
International Tennis Open, Nice and Monaco
Ski Grand Prix, Isola 2000
Procession of the Dead Christ, Roquebrune-Cap-Martin (Maundy Thursday/Good Friday)

May
Cannes Film Festival (2nd week ➤ 55)
Fête de la Rose, Grasse (2nd weekend)
Bravade de Saint-Torpes, St-Tropez (16–18 May ➤ 83)
International Formula One Grand Prix, Monaco

June
Sacred Music Festival, Nice
Procession dai Limaça – snail Festival, Gorbio
Bravade des Espagnols, St-Tropez (15 Jun)

July
Nice Jazz Festival (first two weeks)
International Art Festival, Cagnes
Festival Américain, Cannes (4–14 Aug)
Nikaïa – International Athletics Meeting, Nice
Fête Nationale – Bastille Day fête with fireworks and flower battles, Nice (14 Jul)
Fête de Saint-Pierre, with water jousting, Cap d'Antibes (second Sunday)
Modern Music Festival, St-Paul-de-Vence (Jul–Aug)
Summer Jazz Festival, Juan-les-Pins (two weeks)
International Fireworks Festival, Monaco (Jul–Aug)
Numerous arts festivals at Beaulieu-sur-Mer, Menton, St-Paul-de-Vence, Vence and other towns and villages

August
Jazz and Theatre Festival, Ramatuelle (➤ 85)
Chamber Music Festival, Menton
Jasmine Festival, Grasse (first Sun)
Passion Procession, Roquebrune (5 Aug)

September
Festin des Baguettes, Peille
Triathlon de Nice
Nioulargue Yacht Regatta, St-Tropez (end Sep–1st week Oct)

October
Pays de Fayence Music Festival (➤ 57)

November
Expo-Cannes (Nov/Dec)

December
Bain de Noël – Christmas skinny-dipping in the Med (25 Dec)

Practical Matters

Above: *children boating in Monte-Carlo*
Below: *Vallauris is famous for its pottery*

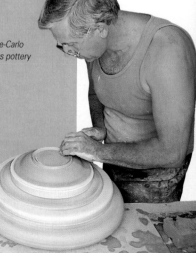

TIME DIFFERENCES

GMT 12 noon	→ **France** 1PM	→ **Germany** 1PM	← **USA (NY)** 7AM	→ **Netherlands** 1PM	→ **Spain** 1PM

BEFORE YOU GO

WHAT YOU NEED

- ● Required
- ○ Suggested
- ▲ Not required

	UK	Germany	USA	Netherlands	Spain
Passport/National Identity Card	●	●	●	●	●
Visa	▲	▲	▲	▲	▲
Onward or return ticket	▲	▲	▲	▲	▲
Health inoculations	▲	▲	▲	▲	▲
Health documentation (reciprocal agreement document (► 123, Health)	●	●	▲	●	●
Travel insurance	○	○	○	○	○
Driving licence (national)	●	●	●	●	●
Car insurance certificate (of own car)	○	○	○	○	○
Car registration document (if own car)	●	●	●	●	●

WHEN TO GO

French Riviera

| High season |
| Low season |

12°C	12°C	14°C	18°C	21°C	27°C	28°C	28°C	25°C	22°C	17°C	14°C
JAN	FEB	MAR	APR	MAY	JUN	JUL	AUG	SEP	OCT	NOV	DEC

 Very wet   Wet   Cloud   Sun

TOURIST OFFICES

In the UK
French Tourist
Office
178 Piccadilly
London W1V 0AL
☎ 0891 244123
(recorded
information)

Monaco
Government Tourist
and Convention
Office
The Chambers
Chelsea Harbour
London SW10 0XF
☎ 0500 006114

In the USA
French Government
Tourist Office
444 Madison
Avenue, 16th floor
New York
NY 10022
☎ 212/838 7800

Monaco
Government Tourist
and Convention
Bureau
565 Fifth Avenue,
23rd floor
New York
NY10017
☎ 800/753 9696

POLICE 17

FIRE 18

AMBULANCE 15

SOS TRAVELLERS 04 91 62 12 80

WHEN YOU ARE THERE

ARRIVING

The national airline, Air France (☎ 0802 802 802 in France) has scheduled flights to Nice-Côte d'Azur Airport from Britain, mainland Europe and beyond. French Railways (SNCF) operate high speed trains (TGV) from Paris to main Riviera stations.

Nice-Côte d'Azur Airport	Journey times	
Kilometres to city centre	🚊	N/A
	🚆	20 minutes
7 kilometres	🚌	15 minutes

MONEY

The monetary unit of France and Monaco is the French franc (FF), which is divided into 100 centimes.

There are coins of 5, 10, 20 and 50 centimes and 1, 2, 5, 10 and 20 francs.
Notes are issued in 20, 50, 100, 200 and 500 francs.

Monaco has its own coins of the same value as French coins also in circulation, but they are not generally accepted outside the Principality.

On 1 January 1999 the euro became the official currency of France, and the French franc became a denomination of the euro. French franc notes and coins continue to be legal tender during a transitional period. Euro bank notes and coins are likely to start to be introduced by 1 January 2002.

TIME

France is one hour ahead of Greenwich Mean Time (GMT+1), but from late March, when clocks are put forward one hour, until late October, French summer time (GMT+2) operates.

CUSTOMS

 YES

Goods obtained Duty Free Inside the EU or goods bought outside the EU (Limits):
Alcohol (over 22% vol): 1L or
Alcohol (not over 22% vol): 2L and
Still table wine: 2L
Cigarettes: 200 or Cigars: 50 or Tobacco: 250gms
Perfume: 60ml
Toilet water: 250ml
Goods bought Duty and Tax Paid for own use inside the EU (Guidance Levels):
Alcohol (over 22% vol): 10L
Alcohol (not over 22% vol): 20L and Wine (max 60L sparkling): 90L Beer: 110L
Cigarettes: 800, Cigars: 200, Tobacco: 1kg
Perfume and Toilet water: no limit

You must be 17 or over to benefit from the alcohol and tobacco allowances.

 NO

Drugs, firearms, ammunition, offensive weapons, obscene material, unlicensed animals.

119

EMBASSIES AND CONSULATES

UK	Germany	USA	Netherlands	Spain
04 93 82 32 04 (N)	04 93 83 55 25 (N)	04 93 88 89 55 (N)	04 93 87 52 94 (N)	04 93 30 24 98 (N)
377/93 50 99 66 (M)	377/ 93 30 19 49 (M)		377/ 92 05 15 02 (M)	377/ 93 30 24 98 (M)

Key: (N) – Nice; (M) – Monaco

WHEN YOU ARE THERE

TOURIST OFFICES

Regional Office

- Comité Régional de Tourisme Riviera Côte d'Azur
  5 promenade des Anglais
  BP 602
  06011 Nice
  ☎ 04 93 87 60 60
  Fax: 04 93 16 85 16

Local Tourist Offices

Cannes

- Syndicat d'Initiative
  Palais des Festivals
  esplanade du Président-Georges-Pompidou
  Cannes
  ☎ 04 93 39 24 53

Monaco

- Direction du Tourisme et des Congrès de la Principauté de Monaco
  2a boulevard des Moulins
  Monte-Carlo
  MC98030 Monaco Cedex
  ☎ 377/92 16 61 66

Nice

- Office du Tourisme et des Congrès
  Feber (near airport)
  promenade des Anglais
  ☎ 04 93 83 32 64
  Fax: 04 93 72 08 27

St-Tropez

- Office du Tourisme
  quai Jean Jaurès
  BP 183
  83992 St-Tropez
  ☎ 04 94 97 45 21

NATIONAL HOLIDAYS

J	F	M	A	M	J	J	A	S	O	N	D
2		1(2)	(1)	2(3)	1(1)	1	1			3	2

1 Jan	New Year's Day
27 Jan	St-Dévote's Day (Monaco only)
Mar/Apr	Easter Sunday and Monday
1 May	Labour Day
8 May	VE Day (France only)
May/Jun	Whit Sunday and Monday
Jun	Corpus Christi (Monaco only)
14 Jul	Bastille Day (France only)
15 Aug	Assumption
1 Nov	All Saints' Day
11 Nov	Remembrance Day (France only)
19 Nov	Monaco National Holiday (Monaco only)
9 Dec	Immaculate Conception (Monaco only)
25 Dec	Christmas Day

OPENING HOURS

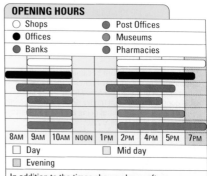

○ Shops   ● Post Offices
● Offices   ● Museums
● Banks   ● Pharmacies

| 8AM | 9AM | 10AM | NOON | 1PM | 2PM | 4PM | 5PM | 7PM |

☐ Day   ☐ Mid day
☐ Evening

In addition to the times shown above, afternoon opening times of shops in summer is 4 to 8 or 9PM. Most shops close on Sunday and many on Monday. Small food shops open from 7:30AM and may open on Sunday morning. Large department stores do not close for lunch and hypermarkets open 10–9 or 10–10 but may shut on Monday morning. Banks are closed on Sunday as well as Saturday or Monday.
Some museums and monuments have extended summer hours. Many close on one day a week: either Monday (municipal ones) or Tuesday (national ones).

DRIVE ON THE RIGHT

TOILETS CHARGE

PUBLIC TRANSPORT

 Internal Flights Air Inter – information via Air France (► 119, Arriving) and travel agents – is the French internal airline, linking 45 cities and towns, among them Nice, Cannes and Fréjus. Some private airlines serve smaller towns.

Trains The main line of the Riviera links the main towns and cities with the Rhône Valley. A spectacular stretch runs behind the coast from Fréjus/St-Raphaël to Menton, which in summer is the most efficient way to travel along this busy stretch of coastline.

Area Buses Services run by a number of private companies are punctual and comfortable, but not very frequent outside main urban areas and coastal resorts. There are also SNCF buses, which serve places on rail routes where trains do not stop. For further information, contact Nice bus station (☎ 04 93 85 61 81).

Island Ferries One of the best ways to explore the Riviera's coastline is by boat. There are frequent ferries to the nearby Îles de Lérins from Cannes, a coastal service between le Lavandou, Cavalaire-sur-Mer, St-Tropez and Ste-Maxime in summer (contact local tourist offices for details), and daily sailings to Corsica from the Vieux Port (Old Port) of Nice.

Urban Transport Most sizeable towns have a bus station (*gare routière*), often near the railway station. Services, even in cities, stop about 9PM. The most efficient bus network is in Nice, where computerised signboards at every bus-stop inform you of the exact time of arrival of your service.

CAR RENTAL

 Main car-rental companies have desks at Nice-Côte d'Azur Airport and in the main towns. Car hire is expensive, but airlines and tour operators offer fly-drive, and French Railways (SNCF) train/car packages, which are often more economical.

TAXIS

 Taxis are very expensive and not allowed to cruise. They must pick up at ranks (*stations de taxi*) found at airports, railway stations and elsewhere. Always check there is a meter. There is a pick-up charge plus a rate per minute – check with the driver.

DRIVING

 Speed limit on motorways (auto-routes): **130kph** (50kph in poor visibility). Speed limit on dual carriageways: **110kph**

 Speed limit on main roads: **90kph**

 Speed limit on minor roads: **50kph**

 Must be worn in front seats at all times and in rear seats where fitted.

 Limit: 0.05 per cent alcohol per litre of blood.

 Petrol (*essence*) including unleaded (*sans plomb*) is widely available. Petrol stations are numerous along main roads but rarer in mountainous areas. Some on minor roads are closed on Sunday. Most take credit cards. Maps showing petrol stations are available from main tourist offices.

 A red warning triangle must by carried if your car has no hazard warning lights, but it is advised for all motorists. Place this 30m behind the car in the event of an accident or breakdown. On motorways ring from emergency phones (every 2km) to contact the local breakdown service. Off motorways, the police will advise on local breakdown services.

PERSONAL SAFETY

The *Police Municipale* (blue uniforms) carry police duties in cities and towns. The *Gendarmes* (blue trousers, black jackets, white belts), the national police force, cover the countryside and smaller places. The *CRS* deal with emergencies and also look after safety on beaches. Monaco has its own police.

To help prevent crime:
- Do not use unmanned roadside rest areas at night
- Do not carry more cash than you need
- Do not leave valuables on the beach or poolside
- Beware of pickpockets in crowded places
- Avoid walking alone in dark alleys at night
- Cars should be secured.

Police assistance:
☎ **17** from any call box

TELEPHONES

All telephone numbers in France have ten digits (eight in Monaco). There are no area codes except for Monaco (377 precedes the number when phoning from outside the principality). Coins required: 50 centimes, 1, 5 or 10 francs. Phone cards (*télécartes*) are sold in units of 50 or 120 in post offices, tobacconists and newsagents.

International Dialling Codes

From France and Monaco to:	
UK:	00 44
Germany	00 49
USA and Canada:	00 1
Netherlands:	00 31
Spain:	00 34

POST

The PTT (*Poste et Télécommunications*) deals with mail and telephone services. Offices open from 8AM–7PM (12 Sat, closed Sun)

Outside main centres, post offices open shorter hours and may close 12–2. Letter boxes are yellow.

☎ 04 93 82 65 00 (Nice)
☎ 377/93 25 11 11 (Monaco)

ELECTRICITY

The power supply in France is 220 volts.

Type of socket: round, two-hole sockets taking two-round-pin (or occasionally three-round-pin) plugs. British visitors should bring an adaptor; US visitors need a voltage transformer.

TIPS/GRATUITIES

Yes ✓ No ✗		
Restaurants (service incl; tip optional)	✓	
Cafés/bars (service incl; tip optional)	✓	
Hotels (service incl; tip optional)	✓	
Tour guides	✓	F 5/10
Hairdressers	✓	F 5/10
Taxis	✓	F 5/10
Porters	✓	F 5/10
Cloakroom/toilets attendants	✓	small change
Theatre/cinema usherettes	✓	F 5/10

When and What to photograph Hilltop monasteries, charming mountain villages and attractive harbours, soaked in a magical, incandescent light. The Mediterranean summer sun can be powerful at the height of the day, making photos taken at this time appear 'flat'.
Restrictions Flashlight is forbidden in most museums, galleries and churches.
Where to buy film From tourist shops and photo laboratories. Development is quite expensive.

HEALTH

Insurance
Nationals of EU and certain other countries can obtain medical treatment at reduced cost on production of the relevant documentation (Form E111 for Britons); however this does not apply to Monaco. Private medical insurance is still advisable for all visitors.

Dental Services
As for general medical treatment (➤ Insurance), nationals of EU countries can obtain dental treatment at reduced cost. Around 70 per cent of dentists' standard fees are refunded. Private medical insurance is still advisable for all.

Sun Advice
The sunshine yearly average is 3,000 hours on the Riviera. The sunniest (and hottest) months are July and August with an average of 10 hours sun a day and daytime temperatures of 28 degrees Celcius. Particularly during these months you should avoid the midday sun and use a strong sunblock.

Drugs
Pharmacies – recognised by their green cross sign – possess highly qualified staff able to offer medical advice, provide first aid and prescribe and provide a wide range of drugs, though some are available by prescription (*ordonnance*) only.

Safe Water
It is safe to drink tap water served in hotels and restaurants, but never drink from a tap marked *eau non potable*. Many people prefer the taste of bottled water which is cheap and readily available. Drink plenty of water during hot weather.

CONCESSIONS

Students A youth card (*Carte Jeune*), available to those under 26, entitles holders to various discounts for public transport, museum admissions, entertainments, shopping and other facilities (including meals in university canteens); ask at tourist offices and post offices for details.

Senior Citizens A number of tour companies offer special arrangements for senior citizens; for further information contact the French Tourist Office (➤ 118, Tourist Offices). Senior citizens (aged over 60) are eligible for reduced or free entrance to sights, and those aged over 65 are also eligible for fare discounts on public transport.

CLOTHING SIZES

France	UK	Rest of Europe	USA	
46	36	46	36	
48	38	48	38	
50	40	50	40	
52	42	52	42	
54	44	54	44	
56	46	56	46	Suits
41	7	41	8	
42	7.5	42	8.5	
43	8.5	43	9.5	
44	9.5	44	10.5	
45	10.5	45	11.5	
46	11	46	12	Shoes
37	14.5	37	14.5	
38	15	38	15	
39/40	15.5	39/40	15.5	
41	16	41	16	
42	16.5	42	16.5	
43	17	43	17	Shirts
36	8	34	6	
38	10	36	8	
40	12	38	10	
42	14	40	12	
44	16	42	14	
46	18	44	16	Dresses
38	4.5	38	6	
38	5	38	6.5	
39	5.5	39	7	
39	6	39	7.5	
40	6.5	40	8	
41	7	41	8.5	Shoes

WHEN
DEPARTING

- Contact the airport or airline on the day prior to leaving to ensure the flight details are unchanged.
- There is an airport departure tax of F22 for international flights and F15 for internal flights.
- Check the duty-free limits of the country you are entering before departure.

LANGUAGE

French is the native language. In Monaco the traditional Monégasque language (a mixture of French, Provençal and Italian Ligurian) is spoken by the older generation. English is spoken by those involved in the tourist trade and in the larger cosmopolitan centres – less so in smaller, rural places. However, attempts to speak French will always be appreciated. Below is a list of a few helpful words.

More extensive coverage can be found in the AA's *Essential French Phrase Book*.

	hotel	*l'hôtel*	breakfast	*le petit déjeuner*
	room	*la chambre*	chambermaid	*femme de chambre*
	single (room)	*une personne*		
	double (room)	*deux personnes*	bathroom	*la salle de bain*
	per person	*par personne*	shower	*la douche*
	one/two night(s)	*une/deux nuit(s)*	toilet	*les toilettes*
	reservation	*la réservation*	key	*la clef*
	rate	*le tarif*	lift	*l'ascenseur*
	bank	*la banque*	credit card	*la carte de crédit*
	exchange office	*le bureau de change*	exchange rate	*le cours de change*
	post office	*la poste*		
	coin	*la pièce*	commission	*la commission*
	banknote	*le billet*	charge	
	travellers' cheque	*le chèque de voyage*	cashier	*le caissier*
			change	*la monnaie*
	restaurant	*le restaurant*	starters	*les hors d'oeuvres*
	café	*la café*		
	set menu	*le menu à prix fixe*	main course	*le plat principal*
			dish of the day	*le plat du jour*
	lunch	*le déjeuner*	dessert	*le dessert*
	dinner	*le dîner*	bill	*l'addition*
	table	*la table*	drink	*la boisson*
	waiter	*le garçon*	beer	*a bière*
	waitress	*la serveuse*	wine	*le vin*
	water	*l'eau*	coffee	*le café*
	aeroplane	*l'avion*	ticket	*billet*
	airport	*l'aéroport*	single/return	*simple/retour*
	train	*le train*	non-smoking	*non fumeurs*
	bus	*l'autobus*	car	*la voiture*
	station	*la gare*	petrol	*l'essence*
	boat	*le bâteau*	bus stop	*l'arrêt d'autobus*
	port	*le port*	where is...?	*où est...?*
	please	*s'il vous plaît*	how are you?	*comment ça va?*
	thank you	*merci*	do you speak English?	*parlez-vous Anglais?*
	hello	*bonjour*		
	goodbye	*au revoir*	I don't under-stand	*je ne comprends pas*
	good evening	*bon soir*		
	goodnight	*bonne nuit*	how much?	*combien?*
	sorry	*pardon*	open	*ouvert*
	excuse me	*excusez moi*	closed	*fermé*
	you're welcome	*de rien/avec plaisir*	today	*aujourd'hui*
			tomorrow	*demain*

INDEX

Acknowledgements

The Automobile Association wishes to thank the following photographers, libraries, associations
for their assistance in the preparation of this book.
DIAF F/cover (lady); TERESA FISHER 17b, 23b, 35, 36, 40b, 44b; FRENCH PICTURE LIBRARY
21b, 25b, 52, 83b; HULTON GETTY 11, 14b; ROBERT HARDING PICTURE LIBRARY 7b, 31b,
45b, 56; INTERNATIONAL PHOTOBANK 59a; MRI BANKERS' GUIDE TO FOREIGN
CURRENCY 119; MUSÉE DES BEAUX-ARTS 38b; MUSÉE OCÉANOGRAPHIQUE 24b
(Y Berard); Noah and the Rainbow 1961-1966 by Marc Chagall: ADAGP, Paris and DACS, London
1998 39b; PICTURES COLOUR LIBRARY 26b, 39b; WORLD PICTURES LTD 58b, 59b

The remaining photographs are held in the Association's own photo library (AA PHOTO
LIBRARY) and were taken by Rick Strange with the exception of the following:
ADRIAN BAKER F/cover (Jardin Exotique), B/cover, 5a, 6a, 7a, 8a, 9a, 9c, 10a, 12a, 13a, 14a,
15b, 16b, 18b, 19b, 19c, 20b, 27b, 48b, 60, 61, 62b, 65, 71a, 75a, 76, 78b, 86b, 88b, 91b, 117a;
JERRY EDMANSON 122c; ERIC MEACHER 86d; ROGER MOSS 13b, 22b, 37b, 49b, 117b,
122a, 122b; TONY OLIVER 51b; NEIL RAY 6c, 28/9, 53, 67; BARRIE SMITH F/cover (dolls),
5b, 50, 82; JON WYAND 15a, 16a, 17a, 18a, 20a, 21a, 22a, 23a, 24a, 25a, 26a.

Author's Acknowledgements

Teresa Fisher wishes to thank British Midland; National Express; the Office du Tourisme et des
Congrés de Nice; the Garden Beach Hotel at Juan-les-Pins and Le Mas de Chastelas at St-Tropez.

Managing editor: Jackie Staddon Copy editor: Ingrid Morgan Page Layout: Barfoot Design